THE GREEK TRAGEDY
IN NEW TRANSLATIONS

GENERAL EDITORS William Arrowsmith
and Herbert Golder

AESCHYLUS: Persians

THE GREEK TRAGEDY IN NEW TRANSLATIONS
General Editors: William Arrowsmith and Herbert Golder

Now available in paperback

AESCHYLUS

Persians
Translated by Janet Lembke and C. John Herington
Prometheus Bound
Translated by James Scully and C. John Herington
Seven Against Thebes
Translated by Anthony Hecht and Helen H. Bacon

EURIPIDES

Alcestis
Translated by William Arrowsmith
Hecuba
Translated by Janet Lembke and Kenneth J. Reckford

SOPHOCLES

Antigone
Translated by Richard Emil Braun
Oedipus the King
Translated by Stephen Berg and Diskin Clay
Women of Trachis
Translated by C.K. Williams and Gregory W. Dickerson

AESCHYLUS

Persians

Translated by
JANET LEMBKE
and
C. J. HERINGTON

OXFORD UNIVERSITY PRESS
New York   Oxford

OXFORD UNIVERSITY PRESS

Oxford New York Toronto
Delhi Bombay Calcutta Madras Karachi
Petaling Jaya Singapore Hong Kong Tokyo
Nairobi Dar es Salaam Cape Town
Melbourne Auckland

and associated companies in
Berlin Ibadan

First published in 1981 by Oxford University Press, Inc.,
198 Madison Avenue, New York, New York 10016-4314
First issued as an Oxford University Press paperback, 1991

Oxford is a registered trademark of Oxford University Press

Library of Congress Cataloging in Publication Data
Aeschylus.
Persians : Aeschylus.
(The Greek tragedy in new translations)
Includes bibliographical references.
I. Lembke, Janet. II. Herington, C. J.
III. Title.
PA3827.P3L4 1980 882'.01 80-12896
ISBN-13 978-0-19-502777-8

ISBN-13 978-0-19-507008-8 (pbk.)

10 9

Printed in the United States of America

EDITOR'S FOREWORD

The Greek Tragedy in New Translations is based on the conviction that poets like Aeschylus, Sophocles, and Euripides can only be properly rendered by translators who are themselves poets. Scholars may, it is true, produce useful and perceptive versions. But our most urgent present need is for a *re-creation* of these plays—as though they had been written, freshly and greatly, by masters fully at home in the English of our own times. Unless the translator is a poet, his original is likely to reach us in crippled form: deprived of the power and pertinence it must have if it is to speak to us of what is permanent in the Greek. But poetry is not enough; the translator must obviously know what he is doing, or he is bound to do it badly. Clearly, few contemporary poets possess enough Greek to undertake the complex and formidable task of transplanting a Greek play without also "colonializing" it or stripping it of its deep cultural difference, its remoteness from us. And that means depriving the play of that crucial *otherness* of Greek experience—a quality no less valuable to us than its closeness. Collaboration between scholar and poet is therefore the essential operating principle of the series. In fortunate cases scholar and poet co-exist; elsewhere we have teamed able poets and scholars in an effort to supply, through affinity and intimate collaboration, the necessary combination of skills.

An effort has been made to provide the general reader or student with first-rate critical introductions, clear expositions of translators' principles, commentary on difficult passages, ample stage directions, and glossaries of mythical and geographical terms encountered in the plays. Our purpose throughout has been to make the reading of the plays as vivid as possible. But our poets have constantly tried to remember that they were translating plays—plays meant to be produced, in language that actors could speak, naturally and with dignity. The poetry aims at being dramatic poetry and realizing itself in words and actions that are both speakable and playable.

Finally, the reader should perhaps be aware that no pains have been spared in order that the "minor" plays should be translated as carefully and brilliantly as the acknowledged masterpieces. For the Greek Tragedy in New Translations aims to be, in the fullest sense, new. If we need vigorous new poetic versions, we also need to see the plays with fresh eyes, to reassess the plays for ourselves, in terms of our own needs. This means translations that liberate us from the canons of an earlier age because the translators have recognized, and discovered, in often neglected works, the perceptions and wisdom that make these works ours and necessary to us.

A NOTE ON THE SERIES FORMAT

If only for the illusion of coherence, a series of thirty-three Greek plays requires a consistent format. Different translators, each with his individual voice, cannot possibly develop the sense of a single coherent style for each of the three tragedians; nor even the illusion that, despite their differences, the tragedians share a common set of conventions and a generic, or period, style. But they can at least share a common approach to orthography and a common vocabulary of conventions.

1. *Spelling of Greek names*
Adherence to the old convention whereby Greek names were first Latinized before being housed in English is gradually disappearing. We are now clearly moving away from Latinization and toward precise transliteration. The break with tradition may be regrettable, but there is much to be said for hearing and seeing Greek names as though they were both Greek and new, instead of Roman or neo-classical importations. We cannot of course see them as wholly new. For better or worse certain names and myths are too deeply rooted in our literature and thought to be dislodged. To speak of "Helene" and "Hekabe" would be no less pedantic and absurd than to write "Aischylos" or "Platon" or

"Thoukydides." There are of course borderline cases. "Jocasta" (as opposed to "Iokaste") is not a major mythical figure in her own right; her familiarity in her Latin form is a function of the fame of Sophocles' play as the tragedy *par excellence*. And as tourists we go to Delphi, not Delphoi. The precisely transliterated form may be pedantically "right," but the pedantry goes against the grain of cultural habit and actual usage.

As a general rule, we have therefore adopted a "mixed" orthography according to the principles suggested above. When a name has been firmly housed in English (admittedly the question of domestication is often moot), the traditional spelling has been kept. Otherwise names have been transliterated. Throughout the series the *-os* termination of masculine names has been adopted, and Greek diphthongs (as in Iphigeneia) have normally been retained. We cannot expect complete agreement from readers (or from translators, for that matter) about borderline cases. But we want at least to make the operative principle clear: to walk a narrow line between onthographical extremes in the hope of keeping what should not, if possible, be lost; and refreshing, in however tenuous a way, the specific sound and nameboundedness of Greek experience.

2. *Stage directions*
The ancient manuscripts of the Greek plays do not supply stage directions (though the ancient commentators often provide information relevant to staging, delivery, "blocking," etc.). Hence stage directions must be inferred from words and situations and our knowledge of Greek theatrical conventions. At best this is a ticklish and uncertain procedure. But it is surely preferable that good stage directions should be provided by the translator than that the reader should be left to his own devices in visualizing action, gesture, and spectacle. Obviously the directions supplied should be both spare and defensible. Ancient tragedy was austere and "distanced" by means of masks, which means that the reader must not expect the detailed intimacy ("He shrugs and turns wearily away." "She speaks with deliberate slowness, as though to emphasize the point," etc.) which characterizes stage directions in modern naturalistic drama. Because Greek drama is highly rhetorical and stylized, the translator knows that his words must do the real work of inflection and nuance. Therefore every effort has been made to supply the visual and tonal sense required

by a given scene and the reader's (or actor's) putative unfamiliarity with the ancient conventions.

3. Numbering of lines

For the convenience of the reader who may wish to check the English against the Greek text or vice versa, the lines have been numbered according to both the Greek text and the translation. The lines of the English translation have been numbered in multiples of ten, and these numbers have been set in the right-hand margin. The (inclusive) Greek numeration will be found bracketed at the top of the page. The reader will doubtless note that in many plays the English lines outnumber the Greek, but he should not therefore conclude that the translator has been unduly prolix. In most cases the reason is simply that the translator has adopted the free-flowing norms of modern Anglo-American prosody, with its brief, breath- and emphasis-determined lines, and its habit of indicating cadence and caesuras by line length and setting rather than by conventional punctuation. Other translators have preferred four-beat or five-beat lines, and in these cases Greek and English numerations will tend to converge.

4. Notes and Glossary

In addition to the Introduction, each play has been supplemented by Notes (identified by the line numbers of the translation) and a Glossary. The Notes are meant to supply information which the translators deem important to the interpretation of a passage; they also afford the translator an opportunity to justify what he has done.The Glossary is intended to spare the reader the trouble of going elsewhere to look up mythical or geographical terms. The entries are not meant to be comprehensive; when a fuller explanation is needed, it will be found in the Notes.

ON THE TRANSLATORS

Janet Lembke is the versatile author of *Bronze and Iron: Old Latin Poetry from Its Beginnings to 100 B.C.* (Berkeley, 1973), a remarkable poetic effort to recover and renew the fragmentary poetry of archaic Rome. She translated *the Suppliants* of Aeschylus (New York, 1975) for the Oxford series. Her own original poetry has appeared in a wide variety of journals, including *Arion, The Carleton Miscellany, The Minnesota Review, Poetry North-*

west, etc. Her most recent work is a translation for performance of the Latin lyrics of *Tres Filiae*, a twelfth-century church music-drama, into singable English verse. Since 1978 she has been involved as a volunteer in a creative writing workshop for the inmates of a Virginia prison. Subsequent to raising a family and organizing volunteers for a drug-rehabilitation center, she has served as adjunct faculty member at the Blue Ridge Community College and instructor in creative writing at Mary Baldwin College. At Middlebury College she majored in Classics, and later pursued graduate work in Classics at Boston University. At present she is working on a translation of Euripides' *Hecuba*, also for the Greek Tragedies in New Translation series.

Her collaborator, C. J. Herington, is Talcott Professor of Greek and also chairman of the Department of Classics at Yale University. Before his Yale appointment, he taught at the University of Manchester, Toronto University, the University of Texas at Austin, and Stanford. His published works include, in addition to numerous reviews and articles as well as his own fiction and translations, the following books: *The Older Scholia on the Prometheus Bound* (Leiden, 1972); *The Author of the Prometheus Bound* (Austin, 1970); *Athena Parthenos and Athena Polias: A Study in the Religion of Periclean Athens* (Manchester, 1955); and, with James Scully, a translation of the *Prometheus Bound* of Aeschylus (New York, 1975). Among his many honors are a Guggenheim Fellowship and a joint award of the British Academy's Cromer Prize for Greek. He has also served on the editorial boards of *Phoenix, Arion,* and *Yale Classical Studies,* and as associate director of the National Humanities Institute at Yale. In 1978 he was Sather Professor of Classical Literature at Berkeley; his lectures there, under the title *Poetry into Tragedy,* are now in preparation for the press.

ON THE TRANSLATION

The translator who dares to undertake the *Persians* of Aeschylus confronts what seems to me, for sheer daunting difficulty, the Everest of Greek drama. It is not merely that the *Persians* is chronologically the first extant Greek play and therefore arguably more inaccessible than a later play like, say, *Medea* or *Antigone.* The problem, as Professor Herington suggests in his perceptive

Introduction, is that the *Persians* is, to an exceptional degree, permeated by an archaic world-view whose premises are as remote from modern ways of thinking as the medieval Japanese poets of the Manyōshū or the "death-songs" of the American Plains Indians. We can perhaps *imagine* a world in which everything—earth, seas, sky, stars, even stones—is alive, inspired with a common animistic sentience; and we *know*, in a way, what Herington means when he tells us that "only the permanent will make sense of the ephemeral." But we lack the sense of it in our immediate feelings, our minds and emotions. Which means that we also lack the apposite poetics—that oneness of word with thing, and the god-saturated immediacy and radiance of the ordinary which we find in the archaic poetry of Sappho, Alkman, and Pindar. Lacking those things, we also lack the beauty and bravery which archaic (and also classical) Greeks saw in a mortality which accepted its mortal "seasons" and transience as naturally as the fields accept the sun and the rain. In such a world the conviction of mortality is the beginning of meaning; it is also the condition of the moral sense, of a compassionate *human* community. Beyond the immediate kinship of family and *polis* there is a larger human community based upon the possession of a common fate, a common mortal nature. Exampling himself with the transient life of leaf and flower, each man knows—it is this knowledge that makes him man, makes him moral—the rhythm and fate he shares with other men. Knowing this, he also feels compassion for others in whom he recognizes by his own condition—the common suffering of a common fate. It is this shared suffering, this *com*-passion that the Greek poet here, with astonishing sympathy of comprehension, extends to the Persian enemy who, only a few years earlier, had twice sacked his city and against whom he had himself fought. In this sense the *Persians* is the poet's own amnesty, on his city's behalf—an amnesty enacted before an audience that, perhaps already tempted toward its own later imperialistic *hybris* by a *daimon* as deadly as that of Xerxes, might be instructed by the fate of Persia. Confronted with Persian doom, the Athenian audience might feel—how could it fail to feel?—compassion; it might relearn that restraint and sense of natural limit in mortal transience which the Greeks call *sophrosynē*.

For the contemporary American poet, translating a play of this sort requires a special discipline and unusual loyalty to his text. Not loyalty to the letter (which would produce, especially

in the great keening choruses and the huge heart-breaking thren-
ody that closes the play, merely monstrous gibberish, "as though
one madman had translated another"); but rather loyalty to that
"ensouled speech" (*logos empsychos*) advocated by Socrates in
the *Phaedrus*. Such courage and discipline do not come easily.
The worst threat may be the translator's own poetics, the contemporary poetic penchant for exfoliating images or "beefing up"
the diction in order to produce an acceptable lyric intensity. Unless chastened by knowledge and purposive restraint, the formi-
dably strange power of Aeschylus' poetics and the play's overwhelming aurality are almost certain to be lost. As Janet Lembke ob-
serves in her instructive foreword, the translator is all too likely to
"poeticize historical fact beyond recognition," to "crown the hills
with ships rather than temples," and, by so doing, to disturb the
crucial tension between foreground and background.

What Lembke and Herington have accomplished seems to my
prejudiced eye little short of miraculous. But I know what enormous expenditure of effort and thought and imagination, how
many scrapped versions and revisions have gone into the effort.
And I know, as only a translator of Greek tragedy can know, the
incredible complexity of translating a play as strange and grand
and demanding as this.

Let the reader judge. But let his judgment be conscientious
and, if possible, informed. We ourselves are read, as Walt Whit-
man rightly observed, by the works we read. The conscientious
reader of the *Persians* must recognize from the outset that he is
reading a great archaic play whose dramaturgy, poetics, and religious assumptions are not those of his own age; a play that must
therefore be read with a radically different sort of attention and
awareness. Above all, I believe, he must read with an awareness of
what Professor Herington insists is essential to archaic literature—
the ephemeral in relation to its context of eternity; the mortal
and historical foreground against its divine background of an
ever-living universe. What is required is good peripheral vision;
the perceptual habit of observing the crossing of different per-
spectives, the reciprocal, mutually revealing contrast and final
complementarity of foreground and background. The Japanese
Zen poet who sets a fragile brocade of cherry blossoms against a
blue gorge or the inky profile of a stone peak addresses his work
to a reader who possesses the kind of vision that instinctively relates foreground and background. The reader of Aeschylus must

read with similar eyes. Then he will understand what the poet means when he speaks of a sea "blossoming with corpses,"* or when, as in this play, he shows us the outraged unwillingness of a sacred world to be reduced, as in much modern literature, to the status of backdrop or scenery to Man's arrogant position center-stage. The sacred order, unreduced, reveals itself; it thereby reveals Man, his condition and fate, by showing him where he really stands in the great order of things, in the modesty and transience of human scale.

Baltimore and New York   William Arrowsmith

---

* Compare, for instance, with the Aeschylean image these verses from the Nō play, *Kanehira:* "Horror of naked swords,/ Shattering on bone,/ Scenes of eyes gouged out,/ And shields floating on crimson waves/ Like scattered blossoms. . . ."

CONTENTS

PERSIANS

INTRODUCTION

I BACKGROUND: HISTORY AND POETRY

Aeschylus was there, at the desperate struggle between Greeks and Persians in the Strait of Salamis. That is one of the few certainly attested facts in our poet's personal life.[1] Thus it comes about that the *Persians* is not merely a play but also a precious historical document: the description of the battle contained in its long scene 417-867[2] is in fact the only account of any event in the Great Persian Wars that has been composed by an eyewitness.

Yet it seems important, at the outset of any approach to the *Persians* as a whole, to draw a firm line between a historical document in the sense just described, and a conscious, deliberate attempt to record an event with the system and accuracy expected of a modern historian. Too often that distinction has been overlooked by critics of the *Persians*, with the result that they tend to concentrate disproportionately on the question of the poet's historical veracity or otherwise; sometimes with expressions of near-outrage at his apparent distortions of the history of the Persian Wars and of the Persian court, so far as they are known from

1. It was recorded in a now lost book, *Visits*, by the tragedian Ion of Chios, who was a younger contemporary of Aeschylus and knew him personally; the statement is quoted in the ancient Greek commentary (the "Medicean scholia") on the *Persians*.
2. Line numbers throughout the Introduction, Notes, and Glossary refer to the numbers given in the margin of our translation (the traditional numeration of the original Greek text will be found at the head of each page). It should be noted that at some points in the Introduction, for purposes of close exposition, a literal, word-for-word, version of Aeschylus' Greek is given.

3

other sources. Yet even those parts of the play—a relatively small proportion of the whole—that concern events that Aeschylus could have witnessed personally, should be enough to warn us against expecting from him a cool, objective historical account. He was indeed at the battle of Salamis in the fall of 480 B.C., and yet, for a start, his play imagines that battle from an angle of vision which he could not have literally shared. It is—it has to be—a Persian who recalls, for instance, how swiftly the Greek fleet came into sight at the beginning of the battle (650). Further, no Greek personal names are mentioned either in this passage or, for that matter, anywhere in the entire play; and even the names of Persians, although very numerous, seem to be largely invented or misapplied, there for the sake of majesty and pathos.[3] Particulars about the battle, of the kind that we would rightly expect from a historian or even a memoirist, are remarkably few. The only exception is the exact detail of the numbers of ships engaged (555-64), and even that is probably included to emphasize the miraculousness of the Greek victory, and the error of the Persians in trusting to mere numbers. Otherwise, the account of the battle is so generalized that historians argue to this day even about its precise location in Salamis waters; perhaps only the wrecks of the Greek and Persian galleys, if they still survive where they sank under the now-polluted silt of the strait, can ever provide the answer.

Aeschylus' painting of the event is mostly a matter of selected tones and colors rather than of sharp-edged lines. We are left with a vivid impression of what it was like to be at Salamis on that day. We re-experience the determination, almost elation, of the Greeks as the moment of crisis arrived, the shouting, the rhythmic crash of oars, the masses of warships locked together in the narrows, and perhaps above all the frightfulness of the contrast between the human work of butchery and the serene, sunlit natural background.[4] The brilliance and beauty of that dawn are specially emphasized (627-28); Salamis itself is a "dove-broody island" (507); the islet on which so many noble Persians were battered and chopped to pieces is the dancing-place of the god Pan (727-28, a miniature pastoral poem obtruded into the scene of

3. On these see the preliminary note to the Glossary.
4. Those who lived through August 1914 in France, and September 1940 in southern England, have recorded rather similar impressions of the contrast between nature and the activities of man.

blood); the distorted Persian corpses are nibbled by what the Chorus calls, with an irony almost as painful in our time as in theirs, "the silent Children of the Unpollutable" (936, literally translated). Which, being decoded, means the fishes of the sea.

Thus Aeschylus' vision even of the shattering event in which he actually took part is to a great extent a poet's vision, not an objective historian's. But the greater part of the Persians concerns episodes and places which Aeschylus could not possibly have seen, and about which he could hardly have had much precise information. For affairs and personalities in the Persian capital at Susa, where his scene is set, and for the narrative of Xerxes' retreat through northern Greece, there was no way for a poet composing at Athens within eight years of the event to arrive at the objective historical particulars, even if it had occurred to him for one moment that such research was any part of a poet's trade. For we are, after all, dealing not merely with a poet, but with a classical Greek poet. And perhaps the most important single characteristic of the Greek poetic tradition within which Aeschylus worked, as opposed to poetry as it is usually understood in modern times, is this: the Greek poet consistently strove to set the transient doings of mortals against a permanent universe, a universe of ever-present death and ever-living gods. Unless so measured, the particular human act (whether a legendary event, or a contemporary victory at the Olympic Games, for instance) will scarcely be worth narrating, or even intelligible. Only the permanent will make sense of the ephemeral. So worked the mind of the Greek poet, whether epic, lyric, or tragic, from the earliest times into the late fifth century. (Somewhat so, indeed, worked the mind of classical Greek poetry's ultimate heir and enemy, Plato, with incalculable consequences for all our later thinking; but that is another story.)

It is with this tradition firmly in mind, rather than in the expectation of a historical narrative, that we should probably do best to approach the Persians. On one side of us we shall see, as the poet had seen, an awe-inspiring series of purely human events; but on the other side, a no less awe-inspiring universe against whose laws those events can alone be fully understood. To relate those two is the poet's task, not factfinding.

The great empire of the Persians was new, as empires go. It had sprung into being within the lifetime of Aeschylus' parents, in the middle of the sixth century B.C., and a thousand miles away, in the arid uplands eastward of the Tigris. Then it was that

Cyrus the Great merged the realms of Media and Persia under Persian overlordship. The ancient kingdoms of the East fell to that combined power in swift succession: Lydia in Asia Minor, and with Lydia the rest of the peninsula, including the noble Greek cities along its western coast; Babylon; then, under Cyrus' son Cambyses (reigned 530-522 B.C.), the realm of the Pharaohs itself. By the end of the reign of the great Darius (who succeeded to the empire, after a confused interregnum, in 521 B.C., and died in 486), the eastward limit of the Persian rule lay on the banks of the Indus. Southwestward that rule reached out into the Cyrenaica, and northwestward through Thrace to the border of Macedon, so that Greece was already poised between its jaws. In recorded history there had never been such power and wealth under a single ruler, nor so quickly won, anywhere in the world west of China. What it felt like to be a Greek, faced with a threat of such a scale, can partly be imagined from the opening chant and song of the Chorus in the *Persians* itself (1-136), with their roll call of nations and captains in irresistible onward movement. For a modern, however, so much further removed from the terror of that time, and thus more in need of concrete detail, the most vivid sense of the vastness and diversity of the attacking empire can perhaps be gained from Herodotus' account of Xerxes' review of his forces at Doriskos in Thrace.[5] Here the massed nations of the empire are paraded before us, their equipment being described with all the precision of the historian-anthropologist that Herodotus was. First march the Persians and the Medes, wearing the turbanlike national headdress, clad in iron-scaled tunics and in trousers, and carrying wicker shields, short spears, great bows, and daggers; then Kissians, Hyrkanians, Assyrians (these wear outlandish helmets of plaited bronze, and carry knobbed cudgels), Bactrians, Scythians, Indians (these wear cotton tunics, and their bows and arrows are made of cane), Arians, Parthians, Chorasmians, Sogdians . . . and so the catalogue of exotic names and outfits runs on for page after page of Herodotus. It embraces both the famous civilizations of the ancient East, and also many tribes scarcely known otherwise to history. Of the latter class, to take only one example, are the Aithiopians, who as described by Herodotus must have looked like the jokers of that monstrous pack. These are wrapped in the skins of lions or leopards; they

5. Herodotus, *Histories* VII.59-100.

6

shoot stone-tipped arrows; they carry spears tipped with antelope-horn, and knobbed cudgels; "and when they went into battle," adds the historian, "they would smear half of their body with chalk and the other half with vermilion." It was as if all the known and half-known world, in all its phases of civilization from the Stone Age to the Iron Age, was converging against Greece.

Herodotus demands a brief introduction for himself, since it is he who provides us with the only extant full-length and near-contemporary account of the expansion of Persia and its clash with the Greeks, and he will therefore often have to be referred to in the course of this introduction. His *Histories* (as the title is conventionally translated; "*Enquiries*" would be a more accurate rendering), composed probably between ca. 460 and 430 B.C., are based on wide travels in the Near and Middle East, as well as in the Greek world. The information which he thus assembled about peoples, places, and customs is enormous, and perennially fascinating. He is less strong on the political and military history of the Persians, partly because he was working two decades or more after the events, and to a great extent (it would seem) from oral communications; partly because his informants were persons of very uneven reliability, and few if any of them are likely to have had direct access to the inner counsels of the Persian court and high command. The result is a narrative that will respond, to put it mildly, better to the historical standards of a Tolstoy than to those of Clausewitz or Mahan: Herodotus tends to represent a battle or a political development essentially as a series of personal anecdotes. His account of the battle of Salamis[6] is in fact a very good example of his method. It is almost the antithesis of Aeschylus' account, in that it presents a mass of discrete episodes, mostly linked to personalities, yet leaves us with scarcely any impression of the battle as a whole. But Herodotus remains by far the best source we have for the story of the great Persian invasion, and all too often the only source whatever.

As Herodotus tells that story in his Books VII-IX, King Darius had been actively preparing a massive amphibious expedition against Greece since 490 B.C., when he heard the news of the Athenian defeat of a Persian seaborne invasion at Marathon. On Darius' death in 486 B.C., Xerxes, his son by Queen Atossa, succeeded to the empire; and, after various delays and doubts, finally

6. *Histories* VIII.83-96.

launched the expedition early in 480. The enormous land force crossed the Hellespont by a marvelously contrived bridge of boats,[7] and proceeded round the northern coast of the Aegean Sea. Offshore, in parallel, sailed a great fleet. To avoid the dangerous rounding of stormswept Mount Athos, says Herodotus, it passed through a great canal cut by Xerxes' orders across the base of the Athos peninsula.[8] Moving down the east coast of the Greek mainland, the expedition was only temporarily checked by the heroic action in the pass of Thermopylae, and the accompanying naval engagements off Cape Artemision. It flooded on, through Boiotia and into Attica, where the troops sacked and burned Athens, almost all the inhabitants having already fled. Thus by the fall of 480 the Persians had overrun about half of Greece, and their superiority by land and sea was still immense.

With the crushing defeat of Salamis, the apparently irresistible advance was suddenly stopped in its tracks; it is one of the neatest and most decisive peripeties in history. After a short period of indecision, the battered Persian fleet made off in its entirety for the Hellespont, and Xerxes pulled back his army to northern Greece. From there he himself left for Asia, guarded by a detachment from the main army: suffering many privations, it escorted him to the Hellespont and thence to the Lydian capital of Sardis, where he remained for about a year. Before leaving Attica, however, Xerxes had sent off a messenger carrying news of the defeat to Susa. On its arrival there, the people "were so shattered that

---

7. *Histories* VII.33-37 (the construction of the bridge) and VII.55-57 (its passage by the army); IX.121 (how the cables of the bridge were finally brought back to Greece, to be set up as trophies in the Greek temples). The bridge is also mentioned, with awe, in the *Persians* (96-99, 1177-79, 1192; also 1213-28, where it is criticized as an act of impiety against the Sea).

8. *Histories* VII.22-25 (construction), VII.122 (passage of the fleet through it). One of the most surprising omissions from the account of the expedition presented in the *Persians* is that of any mention of this great engineering work. It certainly existed (traces still survive on the peninsula), and—as almost every other Greek or Roman writer who refers to the expedition has not failed to see—it provided a neat rhetorical counterpart to the bridge: the impious Persian not only bridged the sea but also cut open the land! This omission may perhaps illustrate once again the fact that Aeschylus does not write in the first instance as a historian, but as a dramatist seeking to capture his Athenian audience. Few of that audience at that date could have seen, or perhaps even heard much of, the canal in the remote and dangerous corner of the Aegean; on the other hand, *Histories* IX.121 (cited in Note 7) makes it very likely that all of them would have seen relics of the bridge in one of the Athenian temples.

all of them tore their robes, and cried and wailed without measure, blaming Mardonios (one of the chief Persian generals). And this the Persians did not so much because they were distressed about their ships as because they feared for Xerxes."[9]

But the danger to Greece was not over. A very large Persian army still wintered in northern Greece under Mardonios, and in the summer of 479 it advanced southwards as far as Attica, where it sacked what was left of Athens yet again. A few weeks later it met the Greek army near Plataia, just beyond the northwestern border of Attica, and was defeated with great slaughter. On that same day, Herodotus says, a Greek naval force destroyed much of the remainder of the Persian fleet at Mykale on the Asia Minor coast. The great expedition of Xerxes was thus, at last, conclusively defeated, just about a year after the battle of Salamis.[10]

That swift expansion and abrupt disgrace of the Persian Empire, even when told as sober history, have already the quality of drama; it is not often that the raw material of historical events arrives in such aesthetically satisfying shape. This fact in itself might to some extent account for the appeal of the Persian Wars to the Greek artists of the fifth century. Far more important, however, must have been its moral-religious aspect. For the events of the Persian Wars conformed almost miraculously to a law of our mortal existence which the Greeks had understood since time immemorial: a law which had been respected implicitly by the unknown Bronze-Age creators of many a Greek myth, and which had been formulated explicitly by the archaic poets and thinkers. In its least refined form the law simply entails the visitation of God's ferocious punishment on anything that is unduly great, whether physical or mental. Its starkest extant formulation is put, interestingly enough, into the mouth of a Persian by Herodotus. As Xerxes is debating with his Council whether or not to launch the expedition, his uncle Artabanos argues as follows:

Thou seest how God strikes over-large animals with His lightning, and does not allow them to show off, whereas little creatures do not

9. The direct quotation is from Herodotus, *Histories* VIII.99. For the story of the Persian retreat in general, see VIII.113-20; and for Xerxes' one-year stay in Sardis, IX.107 (here, of course, is a major discrepancy with the *Persians*, which has Xerxes back in Susa apparently within days after the defeat at Salamis, and certainly long before the battle of Plataia).

10. Herodotus describes the Plataia campaign in *Histories* IX.1-89, and the battle of Mykale in IX.90-107.

even irritate Him. Thou seest how He always shoots His missiles down upon the highest buildings and the highest trees. It is God's habit to chop back all things that are over-large. By the same rule, a great army is ruined by a little one, and this is the way of it: God in His jealousy hurls panic on them, or thunder, and so—behold! They are ruined in ways unworthy of themselves. For God allows no one to think thoughts of greatness, except Himself.

As stated by Artabanos, the law is automatic, and moral considerations scarcely enter into it: it applies to inanimate as well as animate objects with the chill impartiality of a law in physics. Even in this form, however, it might be invoked by the Greeks, and no doubt was, to explain the astonishing overthrow of the Persian hordes by a single small nation.[11]

For a subtler version, applying more specifically to humanity, we may turn to many of the Greek lyric and elegiac poets from the seventh century B.C. down to the lifetime of Aeschylus. The poetry of the Athenian statesman Solon, who composed ca. 600 B.C., provides some of the best examples. According to this formulation, individual or communal disaster is not simply due to greatness per se, but to a concatenation of circumstances, partly external, partly psychological. Overgreat prosperity (olbos) or satiety (koros), connected with infatuation or failure of judgment (ātē), will issue in an act of insolence or outrageousness (hybris), which brings destruction (also termed ātē: the ambivalent word can cover, in Greek, both the mental fault and its physical consequence).[12] As will be seen in more detail in the final section of this introduction, the same law, and even to a great extent the same terminology, is to be found in the Persians, above all in the pivotal scene where Darius' ghost explains the failure of the expedition.

The Persian Wars must have seemed to fifth-century Greeks a perfect exemplification of the ancient law of hybris-ātē; almost, one might dare to say, the incarnation of it, on the grandest con-

11. The very words attributed to Artabanos in this passage (Herodotus, VII.10.5) may perhaps be an example of such interpretation. The likelihood that Herodotus or any of his informants could have known the actual words spoken at an imperial council held deep in Persia is minimal; Artabanos' speech must therefore be suspected of being a Greek invention, put together after the failure of the expedition.

12. See Solon, Fragments 6 and 13.9-26 (Greek texts in M. L. West, *Iambi et Elegi Graeci*, 2 vols. ([Oxford, 1972], vol. II; text with English translation in J. M. Edmonds, *Elegy and Iambus*, 2 vols. [London and Cambridge, Mass., 1931], vol. I).

ceivable scale. It is almost certainly for this reason that the Persian Wars, alone among the events of classical Greek history, were admitted into the repertoire of all the major arts. It is a well-known—a crucial—feature of Greek art in all media, visual and verbal, that its regular subject matter was divine myth and heroic legend, not contemporary events or personalities. But the Persian Wars broke that taboo. The great contemporary choral poets had several poems on, or alluding to, the wars, and toward the end of the century the famous musician Timotheos wrote a long lyric on the subject, which is still partly extant; its title, like that of Aeschylus' play, is the *Persians*.[13] Scenes of battle between Greeks and Persians are fairly common on Attic red-figure vase paintings, and occasionally even found their way into monumental paintings and sculptures.[14] Of the three fifth-century Attic tragedies certainly known to have had "historical" themes, two referred to the battle of Salamis, i.e., Aeschylus' *Persians* and Phrynichos' *Phoinissai* (which will be described in the following section): the third, a tragedy by Phrynichos on the capture of Miletos, referred to an earlier incident in the struggle between the Greeks and Persians.[15] It might even be argued that the overwhelming shock of the Persian Wars widened the very boundaries of Greek literature (and of our own) by creating historiography, in the unprecedented life-work of Herodotus. But however that may be, it must be clear from the evidence of lyric poetry, painting, sculpture, and the tragedies of Phrynichos that Aeschylus'

13. The Greek texts of the fragments of the lyric poets are best consulted in D. L. Page, *Poetae Melici Graeci* (Oxford, 1962); for translations, see J. M. Edmonds, *Lyra Graeca*, 2nd ed. (Cambridge, Mass., and London, 1928). The great Simonides, who died in 468 B.C., left lyrics on those who were slain at Thermopylae (Fr.532, Page, 21 Edmonds), on the *Sea Battle off Artemision* (Frr.522-25 Page), and on the *Sea Battle off Salamis* (Fr.536 Page). A lyric poem concerning Marathon, by a now unidentifiable composer, survives on papyrus (Fr.932 Page). For the *Persians* by Timotheos, see Frr.788-91 Page. Pindar twice refers explicitly to the Persian Wars in his surviving works: in the fifth and eighth Isthmian Odes.

.14. We hear of a painting of the battle of Marathon in the Stoa Poikile at Athens, by the great painters Panainos and Mikon. Still extant is the sculptured frieze showing Greeks fighting Persians (supposed by some to represent the battle of Plataia) from the little temple of Athena Nike on the Acropolis.

15. Herodotus, *Histories* VI.21, preserves all we know of the play on the capture of Miletos. The sacking of that great city by the Persians in 494 B.C. was the greatest disaster suffered by the Ionian Greeks in their revolt against Persia. For other Greek tragedies on "historical" themes—none, it seems, earlier than the fourth century B.C.—see H. D. Broadhead's edition of the *Persians* (Cambridge, 1960), p. xvii, n. 2.

choice of theme in the *Persians* is not an isolated phenomenon, nor a surprising one, for its time.

Our play has all too often been labeled a "historical tragedy," as if it really belonged to a separate Greek genre comparable to the Roman genre of historical tragedies, the *fabulae praetextae*, or to the Shakespearian Histories. But the superficial analogy seems to lead to a critical, and religious, and, indeed, historical dead end. It will be far more profitable to approach the *Persians* simply as a member of the genre "Attic tragedy," but one which also happens to belong to a class of fifth-century Greek works—in all media—which accepted the Persian Wars as worthy to be received without delay into the ancient repertoire of the national myths.

II FOREGROUND: THE TRAGEDIAN AND HIS WORK

"Aeschylus used to say that once, as a youth, he was guarding the grapes in the countryside and went to sleep. Dionysos appeared over him and told him to compose tragedy. When daylight came, since he wanted to obey the god, he tried it, and found it easy from that time on."[16] With such charming stories as this the later Greeks sought to repair their ignorance about the poet's career, and to account for a miracle of a quite different order: the genesis in his hands of tragedy as a great art-form. But the really certain facts in Aeschylus' biography are few; they are confined almost entirely to information about certain of his dramatic performances, which seems to derive ultimately from the official Athenian archives. We know that he first produced a tragedy at the Great Dionysia in about 500/499 B.C. This fits well enough with the traditional date given by the later Greeks for his birth, namely 525/24 B.C., which may therefore be tentatively accepted. In that case Aeschylus will have been about thirty-five years old at the time of the battle of Marathon, in which he fought;[17]

16. Pausanias (second century A.D.), *Description of Greece* I.21.2.
17. The evidence for this is strong, although perhaps not quite as certain as the evidence for his presence at Salamis (for which see Note 1). It includes the famous epitaph, which according to some ancient sources was to be seen on Aeschylus' tomb in Sicily, and was thought to be by the poet himself; this said nothing whatever about his poetry, but ended: "The glorious, sacred field of Marathon could tell of his valor, and so also could the long-haired Mede, who had good cause to know." A few late and not especially trustworthy sources add that Aeschylus also took part in the actions at Artemision and Plataia.

forty-one when he at last gained first prize in the tragic contests (spring, 484 B.C.); forty-five when he fought at Salamis; and fifty-three when he produced our play, the Persians (spring, 472 B.C.), which is both his first extant tragedy and, of course, the earliest surviving drama in the entire Western tradition.

At the time of the Persians, nearly two thirds of Aeschylus' career as a playwright already lay behind him (it was only about sixteen years later, in 456/55 B.C., that he was to die in Sicily). Very little is known for certain about the character of his work, or indeed about the tragic art in general, during that long period. The majority of Aeschylus' total output of dramas (at least eighty, and very probably eighty-nine) will presumably have been composed then, although none of the last works is individually datable. Scanning their titles, which have mostly been preserved, and the all too scanty fragments, one carries away the general impression of an enormous range of subject-matter and treatment, and an imaginative and poetic power which scarcely ever seems to falter, however short or mutilated the fragment; we shall see some typical examples shortly, in examining the last plays of the Persians tetralogy. But their character as plays is impossible to make out. All that can be said with reasonable certainty is that at some time before 472 Aeschylus must have taken the important step of adding a second actor to the single actor with whom the earliest tragedians had been content; for a second actor is already required in parts of the Persians.[18]

The only other substantial information that we have about the nature of any tragedy produced before 472 is derived from accounts of the work of Phrynichos, who first appeared in the tragic contests at least ten years before Aeschylus did. The ancient reports about his tragedies agree in stating that they were remarkable for the high proportion and fine quality of song which they contained. One source, a little poem ascribed to Phrynichos himself, adds the element of dance: "my dancing art found me (dance-) figures as many as the waves which the cruel night raises in a storm." At least in its high proportion of sung-and-danced lyric poetry, Aeschylus' Persians is evidently still close to the tragic art of Phrynichos. But the resemblances may not have gone much deeper than that. The ancient Greek Argument to the

---

18. Persians, 417-833 (Queen and Messenger), 1090-1383 (Queen and Ghost). The chief ancient authority for Aeschylus' introduction of the second actor is Aristotle, Poetics, chapter IV.

Persians, which is prefixed to our manuscripts of the play, begins: "Glaukos in his work *On the Plots of Aeschylus* says that the *Persians* was adapted from Phrynichos' *Phoinissai*, of which he quotes the beginning: 'These, of the Persians who long ago have marched . . .' The difference is that there a eunuch appears in the beginning, announcing the defeat of Xerxes and laying certain thrones for the counsellors of the realm, but here [i.e., in the *Persians*] a chorus of elders deliver the prologue."[19] Some difference! In the *Phoinissai* the grand catastrophe was evidently announced in the first moments of the play, whereas in the *Persians* Aeschylus can already be seen employing one of his most characteristic and effective techniques: the building up of suspense and doubt before the catastrophe finally explodes over the actors. Further, the very title of Phrynichos' play (literally "The Phoenician Women"), as well as two of its fragments, indicates that his Chorus was feminine, and non-Persian. Hence, presumably, the character of its singing, and the entire atmosphere of the tragedy, would have been totally different.

Phrynichos' latest recorded victory in the tragic contests was in spring, 476 b.c., and there are some grounds for thinking that this may have been the occasion on which he produced the *Phoinissai*. However that may be, there is no doubt as to the plays produced by the victor in spring, 472 b.c.; the record, preserved in the ancient *Argument* to our play, runs: "Aeschylus won, with the *Phineus*, the *Persians*, the *Glaukos of Potniai*, and the *Prometheus*." An Athenian inscription adds to this the name of Aeschylus' *Choregos* (the term for the citizen who financed the production); it is none other than Perikles, who here appears in a public capacity for the first time in history.

The record shows Aeschylus already following the practice which was standard in the tragic contests for the rest of the fifth century. He competes with a tetralogy: three tragedies, followed by a satyr-play. Not a great deal has survived of any of them, except of course the second on the list, but it is worthwhile

19. The Glaukos quoted in the *Argument* may perhaps be one Glaukos of Rhegion, who wrote about 400 b.c., but nothing else is known about his book (if it was indeed his) on Aeschylus' plots. Nor can we judge just what this Glaukos meant by saying that the *Persians* was "adapted from" the *Phoinissai*. The sole resemblance that he cites is a superficial verbal one, between the opening lines of the two plays (line 1 of the *Persians* runs, literally translated: "These, of the Persians who have gone . . ."); but the differences, as we shall see, appear to be far more striking.

putting together what we know of the dramatic frame within which the original spectators experienced the *Persians*.[20] The *Phineus* concerned the blind seer of that name, who lived at Salmydessos (on the Black Sea coast, northward of the Bosporos) and was harassed by onsets of the Harpies on his food. He was relieved by the twin sons of Boreas, the North Wind, who arrived in the company of the Argonauts; they pursued and eventually killed the Harpies. Next in order of performance came the *Persians*; and then, last of the three tragedies, the *Glaukos of Potniai*.[21] Its title-character was a king of Corinth, whose obscure legend is told in many versions. Most agreed, however, that he died being devoured by his own team of horses during the funeral games held for Pelias. The exact version followed in Aeschylus' play is uncertain, but the fragments allow us glimpses of two scenes. In one, the Chorus is wishing a prosperous journey to a departing traveler, who could well be Glaukos on his way to the games. In the second, preserved in a badly tattered papyrus, a woman who may well be Glaukos' queen seems to be relating a a dream which involves *horses, the nave of a chariot-wheel, biting,* and *dragging*. A Messenger then tells her about Glaukos at the games; in his fragmentary speech there is mention of a *race,* a *charioteer,* and again of *biting.* If the papyrus is correctly interpreted, there were close parallels here to the first episode of the *Persians* (lines 183-867), where also a Queen narrates an ominous dream concerning an absent male relative, the true meaning of which is subsequently revealed by a Messenger. Aeschylus may thus have displayed his characteristic suspense-building technique in the *Glaukos* also. But it is difficult to make out any further connection among the three tragedies produced on this occasion.[22]

20. The only near-complete collection of the evidence for the tetralogy of 472 B.C. is to be found in H. J. Mette, *Die Fragmente der Tragödien des Aischylos* (Berlin, 1959), pp. 158-66. The reconstruction of the tetralogy is discussed at some length by Broadhead in his edition of the *Persians*, pp. lv-lx. There exists no complete English translation of Aeschylus' fragments, but H. Weir Smyth, *Aeschylus,* 2 vols. vol. II (second ed., with appendix by Hugh Lloyd-Jones [London and Cambridge, Mass., 1957], vol. II) provides translations of most of the fragments of any length, with good discussions, in brief, of what is known of the lost plays.

21. The manuscript evidence for the *Argument* of the *Persians* shows almost conclusively that this, at least, was what the Alexandrian scholars believed to be the title of the third tragedy. Modern attempts to substitute *Glaukos Pontios* ("Glaukos of the Sea") for it rest on no evidence at all.

22. Broadhead, in the discussion referred to in Note 20, discusses attempts, mostly by certain nineteenth-century students of Aeschylus, to show that all

The title of the fourth and last play is recorded (as we saw) simply as *Prometheus*. Since the fourth play was normally a satyr-play, it is natural to identify it with the only Promethean satyr-play now identifiable among the fragments of Aeschylus: the work known to the Alexandrian scholars as *Prometheus Pyrkaeus*, "the Firelighter." The fragments of this show that it concerned Prometheus' carrying of fire to earth. In one of them we glimpse a member of the satyr-chorus so enchanted by his first sight of a flame that he tries to kiss it. In another, preserved on papyrus, there are parts of a marvelously lively song performed by the satyrs as they reel around this world's very first bonfire.[23]

So far as we can reconstruct it as a whole, the tetralogy of 472 B.C. presented the original audience with an amazing range both of theme and of tone; the primeval winged monsters on the far-off Thracian coast, and the all too familiar galleys grappling in Salamis waters; the terror of an empire's pride (of *all* human pride?) brought to nothing, and the comic fantasy, light-as-fire, of the *Prometheus Pyrkaeus*. Yet almost from the first, the *Persians* seems to have been singled out in popular favor. Even in Aeschylus' lifetime it received the distinction (unparalleled, so far as is known) of a command re-performance at the court of the tyrant Hieron of Syracuse, which brought the poet, we are told, "great fame."[24] Long after, in the declining years of the Roman Empire, it was included in the selection of seven plays of Aeschylus for school reading, which has been preserved in one or two of our medieval manuscripts. Even a thousand years after that, when the schools of a shrunken and threatened Byzantine Empire

---

three tragedies may have been connected by a single overriding theme, namely the Persian Wars. It seems now to be generally agreed that this theory must be abandoned, or at least shelved; not because it is impossible *per se*, but because the evidence so far available is simply inadequate to justify it.

23. This fragment is edited, with English translation, by Lloyd-Jones in his Appendix to Smyth's *Aeschylus* (see Note 20), pp. 562-66. The attribution of the fragment to the satyr-play *Prometheus Pyrkaeus* is not quite certain, but seems extremely likely. The main objection that has been raised to it is that the singers in the papyrus refer to a *chiton*, a kind of tunic not associated by most people with the uncivilized satyrs; but this objection seems to be disposed of by an unnoticed remark in the lexicographer Pollux, who, describing various kinds of satyr-play dress, includes "the shaggy *chiton*, which is worn by the Silens" (Pollux, *Onomastikon* IV.118).

24. The evidence is given in Broadhead's edition of the *Persians*, pp. xlviii-xlix. This re-performance must have taken place within five years of the original production at Athens, since Hieron died in 467/66 B.C.

cut down the reading-selection yet again to three plays, only, of Aeschylus, the *Persians*—this memorial of a Greek triumph over the powers of the East, this solemn warning about the way life is—remained on the syllabus. So it has come to us, in our turn.

III STAGING AND DELIVERY

The guise in which the *Persians* (like the other six plays of Aeschylus) has come to us from antiquity through medieval Byzantium is essentially that of a bare verbal text. Most of the manuscripts on which we depend offer an *Argument* at the beginning of the text, and some also offer a marginal commentary. In part, at least, the *Argument* and commentary can be traced back to some of the best ancient Greek scholars, working, many of them in the Alexandrian Library, with materials and information that would otherwise be quite lost to us. Every student of Aeschylus owes a great debt to these men for their preservation and explication of the texts. Unfortunately, however, even the earliest of them worked at least two centuries after Aeschylus' death, and in any case their interests were almost exclusively verbal. Either they could not, or they would not, comment to any significant extent on the manner of staging, the masks and costumes, the properties, the delivery, the melodies, the rhythms of speech, song, and dance—in fact, on any of those elements which were combined with the verbal poetry to make up the totality of an Aeschylean drama.

There are two resources available for the modern student of Aeschylus, or indeed of any Greek tragedy, who is seeking, as he or she should, to re-experience that totality—to conjure it up in all its dimensions from these written symbols that lie silent and flat on this paper. The first resource is the general information that has been built up from miscellaneous ancient sources, literary and archaeological, about the Attic theater, its physical layout, its costumes, its music, and so on.[25] Unfortunately, this is less helpful than usual when we are dealing with a play produced as early as 472 B.C. We simply do not know what the Theater of Dionysos looked like only seven years after the second Persian

25. T. B. L. Webster's *Greek Theatre Production*, second ed. (London, 1970), is one of the many convenient general surveys of these questions. An invaluable detailed sourcebook for most of them is Arthur Pickard-Cambridge, *The Dramatic Festivals of Athens*, second ed. by J. Gould and D. M. Lewis (Oxford, 1968).

sack of Athens, although it is a reasonable guess, which will be adopted in this book, that its main elements were much the same as they are known to have been later. There will have been a circular dancing-floor, the orchēstra, and a few yards south of it the façade of a stage-building, the skēnē; entrance-passages, parodoi, will have led from either side into the area between those two. The Chorus' usual territory will have been the orchēstra, while the actors will most often have been stationed in the area between it and the skēnē; but very free interplay was possible in the earliest extant dramas. Finally, sloping down toward the orchēstra and embracing it on the north, east, and west, was the theatron proper, the audience-area, shaped out of a natural hollow in the southern slope of the Acropolis. The few visual representations of tragic actors and choruses that date from as early as Aeschylus' lifetime suggest in general that the costumes will have been gorgeous, and that the features of the masks (worn by actors and choruses alike) will have shared the simplicity and elegance of other early classical art. The masks were not yet the caricatures of the human face that grimace from above the portals of our Schools of Drama.

But here, so far as the Persians goes, the external evidence for the production gives out, and we must turn to our other major resource, the indications obtainable from the verbal text in itself. As in most ancient Greek dramatic texts, such indications are surprisingly numerous and enlightening. It seems that in the absence of the convention of regular stage-directions (which are extremely rare in Greek manuscripts of any date, and in no case can be proved to go back to the original authors), the Greek dramatists took considerable care to embody hints on the play's production in the actual words that they composed for their choruses and actors.

It is clear from allusions in our text (e.g., 1259) that the imagined scene is somewhere in Susa, capital of the Empire. The earlier part of the play is enacted before "this ancient roofed-building" on which the Chorus "sit down" (183-84, literally translated). That is all the poet has told us, and it seems rather pointless to speculate on what, exactly, the ancient building is.[26] We may fairly deduce, however, that in the original production the

26. Speculations are enumerated in Broadhead's edition of the Persians, pp. xliii-xlvi: Council-Chamber? Darius' tomb? (But would this Chorus actually sit on the tomb of the divine ruler, whose eventual appearance strikes them dumb with terror?) The city gates of Susa . . . ?

façade of the *skēnē* played the part of the "ancient roofed-building," presumably being fitted with a bench or step on which the Chorus could seat themselves. A second structure whose presence is required by the text is the tomb of Darius, which is in the form of an earth-mound (1037, note). Just where this would have been placed is uncertain; we ourselves would prefer to imagine it in the center of the *orchēstra*, to allow ample room all around it for the spectacle of the ghost-raising. It any case, it will be noticed that the stage-set of the *Persians* as a whole clearly resembles the set required for Aeschylus' *Libation-Bearers*. In both these plays, there are two structures, a building and a tomb; and the focus of the action may shift from the one to the other according to the requirements of the drama. In the *Persians*, the passage 961-1397 (perhaps even as far as 1469) will be centered around Darius' tomb; the opening scenes of the play (certainly the first entrance of the Queen, and perhaps the entire passage 1-960) will probably be concentrated in front of the *skēnē*; there is no clear indication in the text as to the acting locale of the finale, 1470 onwards, but one might imagine the Chorus advancing from the tomb of Darius to meet Xerxes as he enters through one of the *parodoi*, and remaining thenceforth in the area between *orchēstra* and *skēnē*.

The text also offers several indications as to the personal appearance of the Chorus and actors of the *Persians*. The Chorus were white-bearded (1690), and voluminously robed (1694). Darius' ghost was certainly represented in Persian costume (1060-61, where he is conjured to appear in saffron-colored sandals, and in the national headdress with its peak upright, as only the King of Kings might wear it). It may fairly be assumed from this that the other characters in the play were likewise costumed as Persians, probably with some attempt at accuracy; after all, it was only a few years since Aeschylus and many of his audience had looked at close quarters on Persians, living and dead. Without being unduly fanciful, we might envisage the characters in our play as resembling the figures who can still be seen on the marvelous reliefs of the palaces built by Darius and Xerxes at Persepolis: handsome but austere-featured men, with a superb majesty in their expression and bearing—of a kind which Greek sculptors tended never to assign to human beings, only to Gods.[27]

On close inspection, the Greek text also provides quite detailed

27. A fairly recent short account of the Persepolis palaces, with illustrations and bibliography: Donald L. Wilber, *Persepolis: The Archaeology of Parsa, Seat of the Persian Kings* (New York, 1969).

information about entrances, exits, and stage-properties. For the modern reader's convenience, we have incorporated that information in marginal stage-directions. Where necessary, our textual justification for such directions is given in the notes. Also in the margins of the translation we have noted the manner in which each part of the play was delivered when it was performed in Greek. For a classical Greek drama might vary between three modes of delivery in any given passage, with profound consequences for that passage's tone and tempo. They were *unaccompanied verse* (normally a six-foot iambic line in the Greek, but sometimes also, in this play, a seven-and-a-half-foot trochaic line); *chant*[28] *with instrumental accompaniment* (in an anapestic metre rather like the anapestic drum-roll that accompanies modern marching); and *fully melodic song* accompanied by instrumental music and, usually, by the dance (in a very wide variety of lyric metres). The metres found in the Greek text allow scarcely any doubt about the moments where Aeschylus shifts from one of the three modes to the other. What cannot, of course, be reproduced in a modern English version, are the precise metres which he used in Greek, in all their subtlety, and variety of emotional effect. Yet to this writer, at least, it seems that the composer of the version offered here has succeeded as well as any translator could hope to succeed in allowing the reader to feel the varying texture of Aeschylean dramatic poetry. Not for the first time she has shown that she knows how

To get the final lilt of songs,
to penetrate the inmost lore of poets . . . .
to diagnose the shifting-delicate tints of love and pride and doubt
                    —to truly understand.

IV GODS

It is recorded that as Xerxes was journeying through Asia Minor to take command of his expedition, "he came upon a plane-tree, which for its beauty's sake he presented with ornaments of gold; and he assigned one of his Immortals to be its attendant."[29] This

---

28. "Chant" or "recitative" seem to be the nearest modern equivalents to this kind of delivery, which the ancient Greeks called *parakataloge*; it is clear that it lay somewhere between spoken verse and melodic song.
29. Herodotus, *Histories* VII.31. The "Immortals" were the elite division of the Persian army, as Herodotus explains in VII.83.

incident in the Great Persian Wars, trivial though it must seem at first sight, serves well to introduce an aspect of archaic Greek and Near Eastern religious thinking which has been almost beyond Western comprehension until quite recently (the ecological movements, and the growing realization of the limitations of technology for the ordering of human fate, may have begun to alter things). Rightly or wrongly, the ancient peoples recognized the existence of a divine power and beauty not merely in their heavenly and infernal Gods, but also in the non-human phenomena of the visible world. The art of living was to walk cautiously and reverently among all the forces of this divine landscape, knowing one's place; if not, the law of *hybris* and *ātē* would be enforced. Seen in that light, Xerxes' gesture to the plane-tree might be counted as his last sane act in the course of the expedition. . . .

Aeschylus' *Persians* happens to be the most spectacular example in Greek literature of this ancient attitude to our world. For the attitude was already an integral element in the ancient and complex system of Greek mythology, which other early Greek poems and dramas naturally draw on quite freely; in a play whose setting and characters are entirely Persian, however, recourse to that system was obviously out of place.[30] Hence it is, perhaps, that the ancient world-vision is here most apparent to a modern observer. The non-human world is alive, and all its members are akin. Most explicitly, and most beautifully, this sense is expressed in the Queen's loving description of the offerings that she brings to Earth (lines 979-87), a little lyric poem in itself. They consist of flowers, "children of Allbearing Earth," and also of liquids for

30. Aeschylus does introduce a few Greek divine names into the *Persians*. For reasons of clarity and emphasis, some of them have been replaced by paraphrases in this translation, but the fact is in each case recorded in the notes. The full list of occurrences may be given here (line-numbers in parentheses indicate where a paraphrase has been used): Phoibos, 323 and note; Hades, (1039-42, 1493); Hermes, (1004); Pan, 728; Poseidon, 1228; Zeus, (868), 1198, 1260, 1357, (1481). But such names occur infinitely less often than in any other Greek play, and in most cases Aeschylus seems to introduce them simply because a Greek audience will recognize them with greater ease (better, for instance, to speak of Apollo than of Ahuramazda!). Non-divine names from Greek mythology are even rarer in this play, and each single one of the instances occurs simply as an alternative wav of naming a geographical site; see the Glossary under AJAX and HELLĒ, and the notes on 922 and 1432-55 for Kychreus and Ikaros respectively. There may be a covert allusion to the legend of Zeus and Danae in 106 (see the note there).

Earth to drink (994); in return she will release Darius from the company of the dead, themselves mighty powers (1106-9). But Earth is not always kindly. When the Persians break the law of moderation, of respect for the way things are, she will ally herself with the Greeks to punish them (1301-3). At the terrible crossing of the river Strymon, the Persians grovel in vain both to her and to Sky (809); here Sun joins in the destruction (815-17). Sea, also, is a powerful force in this play. We have already seen her children at their quiet work on the Persian dead (935-36); that might not have happened had they and Xerxes respected the "shrine" of her windswept waves (133), or the "holy" Hellespont and the Bosporos which "streams from god" (1214-16).

Yet those elemental powers at least the Persians could see and consequently respect (as, indeed, can we) if they were not blinded by ātē. Trickier to deal with, and no less powerful, were the *invisible* powers of the universe, whom Aeschylus normally refers to in this play by the vague names of *theos* or *daimōn*. *Theos* may be, and here usually is, translated "god," and this word will not be too misleading—provided we understand in it the nature of the gods as Homer has depicted them, rather than of the God whom we know in the Judeo-Christian tradition. *Daimōn* is very much more difficult to translate. In Greek it can mean anything from a rather passive and impersonal concept, "fortune," at one end of the spectrum, to a personal being who is not merely active but also spiteful, at the other. In its sense "fortune," and also in the middle bands of the spectrum, *daimōn* roughly overlaps with the possible senses of *theos* (the dead Darius, for instance, is *daimōn* in the Greek text of 1030, but *theos* in 1031): at the opposite end from "fortune," however, it may almost approach the sense of its modern derivative, "demon." There is no word of comparable range in English, and various paraphrases have therefore been used in the translation. Notable passages in which Aeschylus' word is *daimōn* will be found in the translation at 567 ("some Power"), 581, 764, 834-37 (here the *daimōn* jumps down on the Persians with both feet!), 1180 ("Something divine"), 1181, 1474 ("undying Lust for human flesh"), 1489.

And yet, vague and variable as the nomenclature of divinity here is, in any of its visible or invisible manifestations, there seems to be one function that is shared by everything that is divine: it will enforce the ancient law of *hybris* and *ātē*.

V THE TRAGEDY OF THE PERSIANS

It seems that the *Persians* is best understood, both in its structural and in its religious aspects, if it is viewed primarily as *a progressive revelation of divinity* (in the sense explained in section IV) *and of its law*. As the means toward this revelation, Aeschylus orchestrated all the resources at the disposal of an early Attic tragedian: the entire heritage of pre-tragic Greek poetry, song, and dance; and also the new, visual element, which was the crucial innovation of the tragedians. The visual resource, however, he husbanded, just as he does in all his extant plays. He reserves it mostly for the middle and the finale of his *Persians*, with shattering effect.

The audience, no doubt, was (and is) impressed at the outset by the magnificent appearance of the Chorus of Persian Counsellors, and by the pomp of the entrance of the Persian Queen. In that sense, the visual resource of tragedy is drawn on from the beginning. And yet, in the actual development of the drama from its first line through more than half its course, it is *words* that count. The spectator of Aeschylus—more than the spectator of any later classical tragedy, and infinitely more than the spectator of most modern drama—must learn in the first place to listen to the verbal poetry, almost with the same attention that he would give to polyphonic music. For it is in the words that the dramatic themes are usually first developed and interlaced. The eye will have its turn later.

The play's sole great reversal—its peripety, if you will—occurs in the first speech of the Messenger at 417-25, the (in Greek) seven monumental lines which announce the defeat at Salamis. It is an excellent lesson in Aeschylean verbal dramaturgy to follow out the means whereby both the message and the appalling shock which it contains have been quietly prepared for from the first words of the play. Here is a translation of the first four lines of that Messenger-speech (literally translated, for the sake of exact verbal exposition; the same will be true of most of the other phrases quoted in the following paragraphs):

O cities of *all the Asian* land!
O *Persian soil*, and abounding harbor of *wealth!*
How in one stroke has been destroyed the abounding
prosperity, and the *flower of the Persians has gone*, fallen!

Now the phrases italicized are not here for the first time in the play. They, and related phrases, have been uttered before both by the Chorus and by the Queen—not, however, with this horrifying finality, but in shifting tones of love, and pride, and doubt. In the Messenger's speech the phrase "has gone" is the decisive one, which clinches the awful truth (if any doubt were left, it would be removed by the added "fallen"). Commentators have long noticed that the verb used in Greek, *oichomai*, has an inherent double sense; either neutral, "has departed," or abominable "is dead-and-gone, is done for." That same verb is heard in the first line of the play, "These, of the Persians who have gone"; and again in 15-16, "for all the Asian-born might has gone"; and in 81-83, "such is the flower of the men of the Persian soil that has gone"; and in 271-73 (the Queen is speaking), "since my son . . . has gone." In two of these passages the verb *oichomai* is coupled with other phrases which are echoed in the Messenger's first lines: "all the Asian-born might," "flower . . . of the Persian soil." Further, the Persian "wealth," *ploutos*, and prosperity, *olbos*, in the Messenger's speech echo an ominous meditation on these themes which is put into the Queen's mouth at 228-47 ("lest great *ploutos* . . . kick over the *olbos* which Darius won . . . our *ploutos* is beyond blame").

Thus the Messenger's first speech gathers up all the aspects of the Persian Empire which have emerged ambiguously so far in the play—wealth, majesty, command over all Asia, towering pride, and persistent doubts about the doom inherent in all these things—and in one final phrase, "has gone, fallen," determines the true meaning of them all.

This is but one example of Aeschylus' thematic use of words in the *Persians*. Once alerted, the modern reader (who must also, with this poet, learn to be hearer and visualizer too) will find many more, which so far as conditions allow have been brought out in the translation. Some of the phrases which we have already observed will re-echo later in the play, if with less shocking effect: the "Persians' flower," at the eventual appearance of Xerxes himself (1496), and perhaps also in Darius' great metaphorical formulation of the *hybris-ātē* law (1347-49); the "abounding harbor of wealth," in Darius' fear for his "abounding toil of wealth" (1232-33). Other verbal themes which are worth listening for are the pervasive gleam of gold in the Chorus' opening chant (here the resonant Homeric word *polychrysos*, "much-golden," occurs

four times within fifty lines, but is never found again in the
Persians or in the rest of Aeschylus); the sinister word-game,
throughout the tragedy, with the antithesis *fullness-emptiness;*
the *yoke;* and *clothing.* To this last we shall have to return at a
later stage in our account of the tragedy, for it is an example of
the technique—brought to perfection long after, in the *Oresteia—*
whereby Aeschylus may develop an ambiguous verbal theme,
ultimately, into an all too clear visual epiphany.

The Messenger's appearance brings to an end the first of the
play's four major movements,[31] which has built up a picture of
the great wealth and power of the Persian Empire, and of its vulnerability to the laws of the universe (for this last, see above all
137-48; also 225-45, and the dream and omen narrated in 270-
338). The second movement (417-960), like the first, is essentially
verbal and descriptive. It begins from the Messenger's definitive
announcement of disaster; and thereafter is occupied with present-
ing the full dimensions of that disaster, both objectively, in the
words of the Messenger, and emotionally, in the reactions of the
Queen and Chorus.

When the Messenger leaves the scene toward the end of that
second movement, the tragedy has run for almost half its total
length. During that time the Persian Empire has been both built
up and torn down, through poetry of tremendous power. But two
points should be noticed: the effects so far have been overwhelmingly verbal (reinforced, it is true, to an unreconstructible degree,
by melody and dancing in the choral passages); and the story has
been presented entirely at the human level, and through human
eyes. Humanly speaking, the tragedy of Salamis is all over, bar
the wailing, by 833; and that without a single dramatic spectacle,
or even dramatic episode, in the sense that "dramatic" is now-
adays understood. But to a composer and an audience still living
within the ancient poetic tradition, the human action is only one
half of the tally. There can be no completeness until that action
has been seen and interpreted against the background of divinity.

That is the function of the third movement, from the re-entry
of the Queen at 961, through the conjuring and the epiphany of
Darius' Ghost, to the point where he sinks back into the tomb-

---

31. By "movement" we refer to the principal divisions of the play's *content.*
These divisions do not closely coincide with the traditional divisions of a
Greek tragedy by *meter—parodos, episode, kommos,* and so on—which will
be pointed out in our notes to the translation.

mound at 1383. With this movement, the entire texture and technique of the *Persians* changes. The focus of the actors' and audience's attention shifts from the ancient building (i.e. the *skēnē?*) to the tomb (in the center of the *orchēstra?*); the divine world is opened wide, in terrifying majesty; and the visual element in Aeschylus' dramaturgy at long last is brought into full play and will remain so until the end of the drama. It is no great exaggeration (and if there is exaggeration at all, it may be pardoned as an attempt to emphasize a crucial aspect of Aeschylus' art) to suggest that an Athenian spectator who had the misfortune to be stone deaf would have made out, at best, only the general drift of the first two movements; but that from 961 onward he would have been able to follow the *Persians* with increasing assurance, until at the finale he would scarcely be at a disadvantage compared with the rest of the audience.

Central to this third movement is of course the noble figure of the Ghost of Darius, clothed in the full regalia of a Persian monarch. In three aspects Darius makes his impact on the drama: as successful father of the incompetent son Xerxes; as symbol of the splendor of that great empire which Xerxes has shattered; and above all, as one who in death has joined the Gods, and thus can expound the significance of what has happened with divine knowledge and authority. In passing, he also adds yet more to the unhappiness of his hearers (and to the historical coverage of the *Persians*), for he prophesies the great defeat by land which is still to come at Plataia. But the central message of this scene seems to be of universal import. In part it is a magnificent restatement of the old law of *hybris* and *ātē*. The bones of the dead piled high on the field of Plataia, the Ghost says, "will be a wordless signal to the eyes of mankind that, if you are human, your thoughts must not be over-high; *hybris*, flowering out, bears the wheat-ear of *ātē*, and from there reaps a harvest, all of tears" (1344-49, literally translated). The great expedition, in the end, ran up against the way things are. To those who would probe further, and would ask about the personal responsibility of Xerxes for the breaking of the law, the scene responds with a riddle. "Some one of the *daimones*, I dare say, joined with his will," says the Queen, speaking of Xerxes' bridging the Bosporos; to which the Ghost responds, paradoxically, "Ah, yes: it was a great *daimon* that came upon him, so that he should not have right thoughts" (1180-81, literally translated). At 1204-6 the Ghost puts it yet another way: "but when a man himself is eager, the *theos* too joins in."

Spirit or man? Circumstance or individual will? Whether or not Aeschylus knew of the philosophy of his older contemporary Herakleitos of Ephesos (*floruit* ca. 500 B.C.), there can be no proving; but there is a remarkable similarity here to Herakleitos' three-word enigma:

ēthos	*anthropōi*	*daimōn*
"Character	for-man	Destiny"

There is no verb here. Man sits in the middle, in the Greek dative case, the case of the recipient. On either side of him, each in the nominative case, loom Character and Destiny. Question: which of those two is subject, which is predicate? "Character for Man is Destiny?" or "Destiny for Man is Character?" Greek idiom will admit of either translation, equally. No more than Herakleitos, will Aeschylus provide the solution. At the core of his tragedy is the riddle of human responsibility, as it continues to be at the core of our life.

The fourth and final movement (1398-1714) reverts to the human level. Its central theme is the contrast between the splendor of Darius' Empire, and the squalor to which Xerxes has reduced it. The splendor is first recapitulated by means of verbal poetry, in the sonorous choral ode 1398-1469. Immediately on this follows the entrance of a tattered figure, Xerxes himself. In characteristically Aeschylean fashion, the *name* which has echoed through the whole course of the play at last, and at the most effective moment possible, becomes a visible, tangible *person*. Xerxes is set in deliberate visual, and moral, contrast to his father's ghost. From his entry until the end of the play the greatness of the Persian disaster, so far described only in words, is finally brought before the eye.

It is perhaps only at this moment that most spectators will fully realize the extent to which *clothing*, from early in the play, has gradually been manipulated into position as the predominant image of Persian luxury and glory, and of Persian failure. As one thinks back, one remembers the soft, almost subliminal first entry of the theme: the Chorus' fear that they may come to hear the mourning of the women, as "ripping falls on the fine-linen robes" (163). It becomes increasingly insistent and closer to realization, as first the Queen narrates her dream-vision of Xerxes tearing his clothes (315-16), and then the Messenger reports how he actually did tear them when he saw the depth of the disaster at Salamis (756). From the beginning of the third movement, however, clothing moves to the forefront of the action, visually and thematically. The Queen, on returning with the libations for Earth, has changed her adornment from its former splendor (975-76); the Chorus, as we have already seen, conjure the Ghost to appear in the full imperial regalia; the parting words of the Ghost to the Queen, and again of the Queen to the Chorus, heavily emphasize the concern of both for the torn regalia of Xerxes, as if it were the most important thing on earth (1364-97). In the solemn context of national disaster, that emphasis, especially in the words of the Queen (1388-92), has struck many students of the *Persians* as a lapse of taste, and the criticism may well be justified: Aeschylus seems to come perilously close to the borderline between tragedy and black comedy. Even so, his ultimate dramatic purpose in the passage seems beyond doubt. He is preparing us for the ultimate realization of the clothing image, in this fourth and final movement. Here, it is not merely the splendid robes of the Chorus that are rhythmically torn apart to the accompaniment of an antiphonal of terrible lament; it is the imperial majesty of Persia that is destroyed before our eyes.

Looking down the years after the production of this first surviving tragedy in 472 B.C., we see Athens in its turn acquire an empire, and lose it disastrously, before the century is out. During those same years we see a vast upheaval in art, literature, and political and philosophical thinking—a revolution in the mode of human consciousness, the effects of which are with us yet. To the course of that revolution, the successive Attic tragedies, including the later tragedies by Aeschylus himself, are a major witness. As the century advanced, Aeschylus' successors concentrated with increasing psychological subtlety on *individuals*, on their interactions with one another, on their struggles with themselves and with the divine forces which shape (or seem to shape) their personal destinies; and in so concentrating they created an art that is recognizably drama as the world has since understood the term. The gain so achieved is there for all to see and wonder at. Sometimes overlooked is the inevitable corresponding loss. It is the loss of an archaic wholeness of vision, a perception of humanity's place in the great non-human world. Never again after the *Persians* would a tragedy display the fate of an entire nation which clashed with the law of that world. Never again would the law itself be so clearly expounded.

It has quite disappeared from the Attic tragedies which were enacted in the last quarter of the century, under the shadow of the calamitous Peloponnesian War.

New Haven   C.J.H.
August 1979

TRANSLATOR'S NOTE

The story of this translation is partly and appropriately a ghost story. The ghost is not, however, that of King Darius, whose oracular presence commands the third movement of Persians. Instead, a more solid hand delivered a message from the fifteenth century A.D. which gave the work of translation a mysterious and urgent push. It happened this way:

On a warm summer evening in 1975, C. J. Herington exhibited a photostat of the last page of the tragedy's medieval N manuscript (Madrid 4677). That page contains emendations and a subscription in writing other than that of the original copyist. The subscription is signed "Konstantine Laskaris the Byzantine." Some facts about Laskaris' life are known. Born in Constantinople to a princely family, he lived there and pursued the scholarly study of Greek. But when the Turks took the city in 1453, he went into exile, first on Corfu, then in various Italian cities, where he continued to study and teach. It was perhaps not an unusual life, given the times, for a well-born man dedicated to learning. His prime claim to an entry in today's encyclopedias is authorship of a text on grammar, the first book in Greek ever to be set in type and printed. By an odd coincidence, Laskaris' death at the end of the fifteenth century took place in Sicily where Aeschylus himself had died, though in another town, nearly two thousand years earlier.

The N manuscript of Persians is not an authoritative version lying in the mainstream of the tradition from which our current texts derive, but it does have a small, sweet history of its own. Laskaris' subscription is a personal note that tells an astonishing tale:

One must expect anything. For, before the fall of the city, the present very old book—also comprising others of the poets—was, as it were, mine. And, after the capture, finding it in Pherrai, I bought it for a pittance and entrusted it to a certain very good friend along with many other books which—I don't know how—he lost. Then, eighteen years later while living in Messina in Sicily, I obtained it again. I restored it and wrote in the missing parts for the use of those who have nothing better.

Remarkable! Not all the details are clear. Did Laskaris regain the entire book in Sicily or only a part of it? Is the Pherrai mentioned to be equated with Pera, a suburb of Laskaris' Constantinople, or with the location of the modern village of Pherrai in Thrace? It doesn't matter. The basic story is cause enough for wonder, that a manuscript then over a century old, containing Persians and work by poets other than Aeschylus, was lost—twice?—in the aftermath of Constantinople's fall and serendipitously recovered, though in damaged condition, nearly two decades later.

Laskaris' restoration seems to have been a labor of love. And the footnote written in his swift hand became a voice reaching, that summer night, across centuries to issue working orders: Go to it and do your best for the use of those who have nothing better.

The next two years were spent in the fifth century B.C., inside Persians. The text confronts the translator like a rusted tangle of barbed wire, somehow to be straightened out and given a shiny new coat of language. The job cannot be done. For the text of a piece meant for performance is a tiny fraction of the whole; the words are only clues to a host of actions, vocalizations, tempi, pacing, conventions, memories, and emotions that elude print. Where are the actors, the audience, and the currents that once bound them? The absence of all these poses the eternal question of lamentation: Ubi sunt? And because Persians is a work dependent for many of its dramatic effects, especially in the last movement, not merely on verbal meanings but on sounds—sheer, swelling, inarticulate, overwhelming sounds of heartbreak at its most extreme, the play cries out for its lost breath, its forever lost music. How can such a play be re-imagined?

Its message is clear. Pride goeth before a fall; the fall can be bitter indeed. Humankind must check its mortally presumptuous urge to alter and control lest sure retaliation be provoked from Earth and Heaven. These, the statements of *Persians*, are as suited to a technological society as to one of farmers, seafarers, and fighters. And Aeschylus makes them by closing a moment in history within a poetry that is enduring strange and heartrending. The poetry is worth trying to rediscover.

The world of *Persians* is a world that gives no room to metaphor. It is totally alive. Everything human and natural is inseparably linked, and all feelings, all things are potentially sentient and powerful. Fertile Nile flows seaward literally giving birth to Xerxes' Egyptian contingents. Sardis the city actually stands beside the commanders Mitrogathes and Arkteus to subjugate and mount Ionian Greeks in the service of Persia. The plain of Marathon itself is murderous, killing Darius' splendid troops. Care scratches hearts with real claws, and runaway wealth kicks up real dust. The Sea is outraged at being bridged in chains like a slave. Asia falls to her knees. Men flower and are cut down, but in death they may still hear, see, and speak. And the invisible energies of Heaven do indeed have feet and use them to trample the immoderate flesh.

But such marvels and the old acceptance of pervasive vitality are shared by much Greek poetry, especially that on the edge of the archaic. *Persians* is extraordinary for the ways in which Aeschylus combines elements that may now seem to be oil and water, not to be mixed. He mingles the account of a timebound event, the defeat of the Persian forces at Salamis, with magic and the supernatural—a dream, waking omens, soul-raising, prophecy, and the unseen, constant presence of the *daimōn*. Today the play is beyond price as a document of history witnessed. The fact that it is also history dramatized is sometimes viewed as a frustrating blind pulled down on what really happened at Salamis. What, for example, is the identity of the small, nameless island off the coast of Salamis? All the poet tells us is that there, on its harborless rock, Pan dances and many Persians die. The essential drama of the play, however, lies in just such combinations of poetic and historical truths. In the combining the temporal world is surrounded—permeated—by all that is timeless and divine. The tragedy occurs not only on the battlefield and in the wildly lamenting court at Susa; it plays out through eternity. The result is a document of human feeling, a stunning piece of emotional realism. The defeat at Salamis becomes all defeat; the grief spawned there in blood is all grief anywhere at any time.

If the translation succeeds in bringing some of this time-freed drama into the present moment and into playable English, there are living people to be thanked. Not all the impetus behind the work was ghostly. I am grateful to my firm and gentle ally, C. J. Herington, with whom it has been a joy to collaborate. He knows Greek with head and heart. Without his guidance my version of the Persian defeat and withdrawal would have poeticized historical facts past recognition, and ships, not temples, would have crowned the hills. Nor, without him, would the directive from Konstantine Laskaris have reached me.

There are others whose help and participation deserve happy acknowledgment. In the beginning the task of translation was to have been a three-way effort, with the poet James Scully, translator of this series' *Prometheus Bound*, tackling all but the odes, introduction, and notes. The pages he provided gave me a starting point—finding English for the lyrical choral responses to the Messenger's announcement of disaster. Thanks are also due D. S. Carne-Ross, who read an early version of the translation and rescued it from several kinds of unspeakability. Deepest appreciation goes to William Arrowsmith, the first to believe that we might make a *Persians* for our day.

The translation is based primarily on the text edited by H. D. Broadhead, *The Persae of Aeschylus*, Cambridge University Press, 1960. Broadhead's critical notes and commentary furnished many useful explanations of historical, if not dramatic, facts. A second text was also consulted, that of H. Weir Smyth, *Aeschylus*, volume I, Loeb Classical Library, Harvard University Press, 1922. In supplement, two scholarly studies helped me to come to contemporary terms with the ancient art of lamentation. They are Margaret Alexiou's *The Ritual Dirge in Greek Tradition* (Cambridge University Press, 1974) and Gareth Morgan's "The Laments of Mani" (*Folklore*, Volume 84, winter 1973). Professor Morgan was brave enough, too, to give a telephoned rendition of a dirge-tune used today in the southern Peloponnese. And there is one translation of *Persians* that must be credited simply for the pleasure it has given me: the version robustiously made in the late eighteenth century by the Rev. R. Potter, Prebendary of Norwich, and the first to find English verse for the Aeschylean corpus. It is luckily accessible in the Random House collection of Greek tragedies, which may be found in many public libraries.

Throughout its years the work of translation was enhanced by thoughts of two special people. Without any textual justification, I have imagined the Chorus of the Faithful, Persia's elderly regents, as veterans of Darius' wars and fathers of sons gone, and gone forever, with Xerxes' host. To my own two sons, Peter and Charles, young men both at the time of this writing, my translation is dedicated in hope that they will all their lives see days of safe return.

Staunton, Virginia   J. L.
August 1979

PERSIANS

CHARACTERS

CHORUS of old men, regents of Persia
ATOSSA the Queen, mother of Xerxes and Darius' widow
MESSENGER a Persian runner
GHOST OF DARIUS
XERXES King of Persia, son of Darius
Ladies in waiting
Persian soldiers, survivors of the defeat at
Salamis and the subsequent retreat

Line numbers in the right-hand margin of the text refer to
the English translation only, and the Notes at p. 97 are keyed
to these lines. The bracketed line numbers in the running
headlines refer to the Greek text.

An open square in Susa, capital of Persia. In the background, a building reached by steps. Nearer to the spectator, and probably in the center of the dancing-floor, a mound representing the tomb of Darius.

Enter the CHORUS right, marching slowly and delivering anapestic chant.

CHORUS We the old men
　　　　while Persia's young strength has gone
onto Greek soil　　stay at home
　　　　appointed their Faithful,
the lavish and goldwinning throne's
loyal regents
　　　　　　whose age and experience he
Lord Xerxes　　King　　son of Darius
chose himself
　　　　to safeguard his country.　　　　　　　　　　10

King　　royal army　　blazoned in gold
WILL THEY COME HOME?
　　　　　　　　My heart's ragged beat
prophesies doom:
　　　　all Asia's strong sons
are gone　　gone
　　　　　　and now rumors bruit
the young King's name
but not one runner and not one rider
　　　　bring word to Persia's capital.　　　　　　20

They rallied, they marched　　leaving Susa's defenses
　　　　and Ekbatana's
　　　　　　and safe ancient stones that barricade Kissa
some mounted on horses, others on ships
footsoldiers, too, stepping it steady
　　　　eager for combat
　　　　　　man packed on man.

39

You, Amistres
and you, Artaphrenes
you, Megabates   30
and you, Astaspes
Persian commanders
kings in your own right under the Great King
leaders who hurl on the battling horde
you bowtamers, horsebreakers
    chilling to watch
        deadly in war
            because endurance gleams hard in your souls.

You, Artembares, war-joyful horseman
you, Masistres   40
you, the bowtamer shining Imaios
you, Pharandakes
you, too, stallion-driver Sosthanes.

And you
    whose command fertile Nile outpoured
Sousiskanes born in Persia
Pegastagon sundark Egyptian
and godbelov'd Memphis' lord, towering Arsames
and satrap at Old Thebes, Ariomardos
    with swampskippers, rowers   50
        oars dipping silent
            dangerous men, too many to number.

And following close throng
the Lydian thousands
    who relish the rich life
and lord it over every last man
        of the Asia-born race whom
Mitrogathes
and valiant Arkteus
    kingsent commanders   60
and goldladen Sardis
    made to wheel out, chariots clanging

three horses, four, each
a fear-breeding sight.

And pressing on them
Lydia's neighbors
who live in eyes' reach of her godswept peak
Mardon, Tharybis, lance-breaking anvils
Mysians, too, masters of javelins—
all, all have vowed   70
to throw slavery's yoke
firm on the Greeks.

And Babylon the gold-proud
fields motley troops in long horizon-crowding lines
some for a ship's bench
others who trust bowtugging rage
and scimitars from every fort in Asia
surge behind
obeying the King's
deadly orders to march.   80

The CHORUS *come to a halt.*

This
is the flower of Persian earth
the men now gone
and Asia's land that held their roots
groans out loud,
aflame with yearning.
Parents, wives in cold beds
count the days.
Time stretches thin.
They wait and shiver.   90

The CHORUS *begin to sing and dance the invasion of*
Greece.

The army HAS won through! Persians,
Breakers-of-cities, the King's men

            sweep countries lying on the far shore
They've crossed the strait
        that honors Hellē
            by binding their ships
and clamping a bolt-studded road—
a yoke
        hard on the Sea's neck!

And teeming Asia's headstrong   100
        lord has shepherded his flocks
            godsped against the world on two fronts
land and sea
        and trusts his leaders
            stern rocks among men
As heir to a gold-showered line
he gleams
            casting a god's light

But the heart of his eye darkens,
        the death-dealing stare of a snake   110
            Countless its hands!
            Countless the ships!
And he while his chariot sings
        has targeted War's taut bow
            on spearmen trained for close combat

And not one has proved he can stand up
        to men in a ceaseless stream
            nor ever build
            a sure seawall
to stay the unstoppable waves   120
        Resistless, Persia's armed flood
            and the war-joy that crests in her sons

For gods decree
Fate's age-old power here and she
has long charged Persians
with a holy task:
        Wage tower-splitting war

    Hurl forward horse-drawn battle glee
    Lay cities waste

And they have learnt   130
when galewinds lash the saltroad white
to look unshaken
at the Sea's deep shrine:
    entrusting life to slender
    ropes and man-supporting tricks
    they stride the waves

But how crafty
    the scheme of God!
What mere man outleaps it?
What human foot jumps fast enough   140
to tear loose
        from its sudden grip?

For with gestures
    of kindness as bait
Blind Folly fawns a man
into her net, nor can he hope
to work loose
        and escape unhurt

The CHORUS begin a lament, ominous in its prematurity.

My thoughts
    scratched raw by fear   150
        wear black
Shall we wail   WAAAAW!
    for the wide-ranging Persians?
What word for our people?
    That Susa's great heart is
        bled empty of men?

And will
    Kissa's old walls
        din back

that death caw   WAAAAW! 160
   and the thump of the womanhorde
howling and croaking
   ripping fine linen and
      pummeling breasts?

For horseback troops
and troops on foot
   all, all of them
have left home
   in a stinging swarm behind their chief
and all have crossed 170
   the Sea-dividing span
      that juts from two shores
yoking two lands

Here double beds
bereft of men
   are filled with tears
and each wife
   who has rushed to war a headstrong spear
is left to spend
   her gentle elegance 180
      bereft of love, one
yoked but alone

At ode's end the chorus *are scattered, each member*
standing alone to give visual emphasis to the last line.

chorusleader (chanting) Persians! Assemble.
Gather on the steps below this ancient roof.
We should discuss
our carefullest, most deep-debated thoughts,
   for need presses close.

How does he fare
Xerxes   our King   son of Darius?
Where lies the victory? 190

                    Taut bow
or lance's spearing force—
        which one has conquered?

        With her retinue ATOSSA *enters right in a chariot.*

Look up!
        Dazzling as gods' eyes,
a light moves toward us.
Mother of the Great King.
My Queen.

        Prostrate yourselves!
Salute her as adorns her dignity.   200

The CHORUS *prostrate themselves.* (ATOSSA *and the*
CHORUS *speak in unaccompanied trochaic verse from here*
                            through line 269.)

CHORUSLEADER My lady, all honor.
        My lady most blest
                among sonbearing women,
grey mother of Xerxes,
        Darius' wife
                born to share
our god's bed
        and born also
                to mother a god unless—
unless the age-old   210
        Lust for Winning has
                taken itself from our men.

        ATOSSA *descends from her chariot. The* CHORUS *rise.*

ATOSSA Yes, there's
        the reason urging me
                to leave the gold-wrapt
shadow of my house
        and room where once
                Darius slept beside me.

Sharpest care is
    clawing at my heart.   220
        It's you,
good friends,
    to whom I'd speak out
        unvoiced thoughts.
Nothing
    guards my inmost self
        against the fear
that vast Wealth,
    kicking up dust
        as it pelts headlong,   230
may overturn
    continued joy
        in the prosperity
Darius
    by some god's grace
        lifted high.
There's the reason
    an unspeakable, two-pronged
        anxiety sits at my core:
not to bow low   240
    honoring
        a manless treasure-hoard
nor does a light shine
    on the treasureless,
        no matter what their bodies' strength.
Surely our wealth
    is beyond reproach!
        My fear
centers on the Eye,
    for in my mind   250
        the house's Eye
is its master's presence.
    There
        my thoughts rest.
Persians,
    old faithful confidants,
        advise me.

All,
    all my hopes lie in you.
    Guide me.   260

CHORUS Our country's Queen,
      no need
        to ask twice.
A word, an act—
    we'll help if we can
      when you
command our counsel.
    We do intend
      to serve you well.

ATOSSA *(in unaccompanied iambic verse)* Night after night   270
    since my son left with the army he mustered
I am joined with many dreams.
                  He's gone,
  gone to Greece,
    bent on making it Persian and *his*.
But never has a vision showed more clear
than what I saw last night
    in the kind-hearted dark.
I'll tell you:
          It seemed to me   280
two well-dressed women—
one robed with Persian luxury,
the other in a plain Greek tunic—
came into view, both
taller far than any woman now living,
and flawless in beauty,
and sisters from the one same
parentage.
    And for a fatherland, a home,
one was allotted Greek soil,   290
the other, the great world beyond.

         Then I saw
the two of them build bitter quarrels,

one against the other,
and when my son learned this,
he tried to curb and gentle them:
      under his chariot
he yokes the two, and on their necks
he straps broad leather collars.
And the one towered herself   300
      proud in this harness
and she kept her mouth
      well-governed by the reins.
But the other bucked stubborn
      and with both hands
she wrenches harness from the chariot fittings
and drags it by sheer force,
      bridle flung off, and she
shatters the yoke mid-span
and he falls,   310
            my son falls,
and his father is standing beside him—
Darius, pitying him,
      and when Xerxes sees that,
he shreds around his body
the clothes that a king wears.

            I tell you
I did see these things last night.

Today, when I'd risen
and dipped both hands in a clear-rippling spring   320
      to cleanse me of bad dreams,
hands busy with offerings,
I stood by Phoibos' altar
wanting to give mixed honey and wine,
      their expected due,
to the undying Powers that turn away evil.
And I see
            an eagle
fleeing toward the altar's godbright flame.

Frightened, mute, my friends, I   330
        just stood there,
and soon I see a hawk in downstoop
raising wings to break the fall and working
talons in the eagle's head, and the eagle did
nothing,
        only cringed and offered up
its flesh.

                        Terrors! I saw them!
Now you've heard them.
        And you surely know   340
that if my son succeeds, he'll be marveled at,
but if he fails,
        his people cannot call him to account.
When he is safely home,
        he'll rule the country as he always has.

(From here through line 416 ATOSSA and the CHORUS
                        speak in trochaic verse.)

CHORUS Mother,
        here's advice
                meant neither to alarm
nor overgladden you.
        Gods abide: 350
                turn toward them suppliant,
if anything you saw stirs faintest doubt,
        praying them
                to turn it away and bring
goodness to its peak
        for you and
                children in your line,
for Persia, too,
        and those you love.
                Afterward, pour out   360
the drink due Earth
        and give the thirsty dead their sip

and pray, appeasing him,
your husband Darius—
        you say you saw him
            in the kind-hearted night—
asking him to send up
        from his depth into our light
            blessings for you and your son
and hold the reverse back   370
        earth-coffined
            till it molders in that dark.

For this advice
        I have consulted
            my prophetic heart.
Be appeased,
        for as we
            read the signs,
everything
        shall   380
            turn out well.

ATOSSA Yes, you
            the first
                to read my dream,
with goodwill toward my son and house,
        have found
            its true interpretation.
Would that the omens
        turn out well!
            I'll do all you say   390
for gods and old friends under earth
        when I go home.
            But first
I'd like to know, dear friends,
        where
            Athens is.

CHORUSLEADER Far west where the Lord Sun fades out.

ATOSSA My son really wanted to hunt down this city?

CHORUSLEADER Yes, so all Greece would bend beneath a Shah.

ATOSSA Does it field a manhorde of an army?   400

CHORUSLEADER Such that it has worked evils on the Medes.

ATOSSA Then bowtugging arrows glint in their hands?

CHORUSLEADER No. Spears held steady, and heavy shields.

ATOSSA What else? Wealth in their houses?

CHORUSLEADER Treasure, a fountain of silver, lies in their soil.

ATOSSA But who herds the manflock? Who lords the army?

CHORUSLEADER They're not anyone's slaves or subjects.

ATOSSA Then how can they resist invaders?

CHORUSLEADER So well that they crushed Darius' huge and shining army.

ATOSSA Terrible words! You make the parents of those gone
             shudder.   410

CHORUS (severally)
        But I think you will soon hear the whole story.
        Someone's coming!

                    He's ours—
        a Persian clearly by the way he runs.

        Something's happened. Good or bad,
        he brings the plain truth.

                            The MESSENGER enters left.

51

MESSENGER (*in unaccompanied iambic verse throughout this episode*)
Listen! cities that people vast Asia.
Listen! Persian earth, great harbor of wealth.
One stroke, one single stroke has smashed
great prosperity,   420
       and Persia's flower is gone, cut down.
Bitter, being first to tell you bitter news,
but need presses me to unroll the full disaster.
Persians,
              our whole expedition is lost.

CHORUS   (*singing from here through line 469*)
Cruel cruelest evil
       newmade, consuming   Oh
              weep, Persians, who hear
this pain

MESSENGER Everything over there has ended. And I—   430
against all hope, I'm here, seeing this light.

CHORUS   Life stretches long
              too long for grey old men
                     who hear of all hope
       undone

MESSENGER I was *there*. I can tell you, no hearsay,
       the evils that sprang up hurtling against us.

CHORUS   No nonono
              That bright storm
of arrows showing Asia's massed colors   440
advanced
       all for NOTHING
                     into hostile Greece?

MESSENGER They met hard deaths. The corpses
       pile on Salamis and every nearby shore.

CHORUS No nonono
              You're saying
         those we love are floating, foundering
         awash
              DEAD MEN shrouded   450
                        in sea-drowned cloaks?

MESSENGER Our arrows didn't help. The whole force
         went down, broken, when ship rammed ship.

CHORUS Rage
              for the Persians killed
         Wail the death howl
              All that began well
                   comes to the worst end   CRY!
         CRY OUT
                   for the army slaughtered!   460

MESSENGER Salamis, I hate that hissing name.
         And Athens, remembering makes me groan.

CHORUS Athens
              bears Persia's hate
         We will recall
              wives she has widowed
                   mothers with no sons   NO!
         and all
              ALL FOR NOTHING!

         (ALL speak in iambic verse from here through line 867.)

ATOSSA Silence has held me till now   470
         heartsore,
              struck by the blows of loss,
         for this disaster so exceeds all bounds
         that one can neither tell,
         nor ask,
              about the suffering.

Yet there is terrible need
    for people to bear pain
when gods send it down.
              You must   480
compose yourself: speak out,
unrolling *all* the suffering,
    though you groan at our losses.
Who is not dead?
And whom shall we mourn?
Of all the leaders
    whose hands grip authority
which one
    left his post unmanned, deserted
when he died?   490

MESSENGER Xerxes—he lives and sees light—

ATOSSA You speak: light blazes in my house,
    and white day after a black-storming night!

MESSENGER —but Artembares,
        commander of ten thousand horse,
is hammered along Sileniai's raw coast
and thousand-leader Dadakes,
    spearstuck,
danced back without any effort I could see
        overboard   500
and Tenagon,
    pureblooded Bactrian and chief,
scrapes against Ajax' sea-pelted island.

Lilaios,
Arsames,
and a third, Argestes,
    wave-tumbled around that dove-broody island,
kept butting resistant stones
and so did Pharnoukhos
    whose home was Egypt, by Nile's fresh flow,   510

and so did they
    who plunged from one same ship,
Arkteus,
Adeues,
and a third, Pheresseues.
    And Matallos from a golden city,
        leader of ten thousand,
dying, stained his full beard's tawny brush
changing its color with sea-purple dye.

And the Arab, Magos,   520
with Artabes the Bactrian,
    who led thirty thousand black horse,
took up land as an immigrant
by dying there
    on that harsh ground.

Amistris
and Amphistreus,
    whose spear delighted in trouble,
and bright-souled Ariomardos,
    whose loss brings Sardis down grieving,   530
and Seisames the Mysian,
Tharybis, too,
    sealord of five times fifty ships,
    Lyrnaian by descent, a hard-bodied man,
lies dead,
    a wretch whose luck went soft,
and Syennesis,
    first in courage, the Cilicians' chief,
    one man who made most trouble for the enemy,
died with glory.   540

              These are the leaders
of whom I bring my memories.
But we suffered many losses there.
I report a mere few.

The CHORUS *cry out sharply.*

ATOSSA Noooo!
        These words I hear
lift evil to its height.
O the shame cast on Persians,
and the piercing laments!

But tell me,   550
            turn back again,
was the count of Greek ships so great
they dared launch their rams
        against Persia's fleet?

MESSENGER If numbers were all, believe me,
Asia's navy would have won,
for Greek ships counted out
at only ten times thirty
        and ten selected to lead out that line.
But Xerxes, this I know,   560
commanded a full thousand,
        two hundred and seven
        the fastest ever built.
That is our count. Perhaps you thought
we were outnumbered?
                    No.
It was some Power—
        Something not human—
whose weight tipped the scales of luck
and cut our forces down.   570
Gods keep Athens safe for her goddess.

ATOSSA You're saying that Athens is not yet sacked?

MESSENGER Long as her men live, her stronghold can't be shaken.

ATOSSA But at the beginning, when ship met ship,
tell me, who started the clash?
                        Greeks?

56

Or my son
    who exulted in his thousand ships?

MESSENGER My lady,
    the first sign of the whole disaster came   580
when Something vengeful—
    or evil and not human—
appeared from somewhere out there.

For a Greek,
    who came in stealth from the Athenian fleet,
whispered this to your son Xerxes:
As soon as black night brought its darkness on,
Greeks would not maintain their stations, no,
but springing on the rowing benches,
    scattering here, there in secret flight,   590
would try to save their own skins.
And at once,
    for he had listened not understanding
    the man's treachery nor the gods' high jealousy,
he gave all his captains this command:
As soon as Sun's hot eye let go of Earth
and darkness seized the holy vault of Sky, then
they should deploy ships
    in three tight-packed ranks
to bar outsailings and the salt-hammered path,   600
while others circled Ajax' island.
And if the Greeks should somehow slip the trap
    by setting sail, finding a hidden route,
Xerxes stated flatly
    that every last captain would lose his head.
So he commanded in great good spirits.
He could not know the outcome set by gods.

There was no disorder. Obediently
the crews prepared their suppers,
and each sailor, taking a thong,   610
    made his oar snug to the tholepin.
And when Sun's glow faded and Night

was coming on,
                    each oarlord,
each expert man-at-arms
        boarded his ship.
Squadron on squadron, cheers for the warships
roared from the decks,
                    and they sailed,
each captain maintaining his position.   620
And all night long the lords of the fleet
kept fully manned vessels plying the channel.
And night was wearing on.
                            The Greek forces never
tried sailing out secretly.
Not once.

But when Day rode her white colt
dazzling the whole world,
                        the first thing we heard
was a roar, a windhowl, Greeks   630
singing together, shouting for joy,
and Echo at once hurled back
that warcry
        loud and clear from island rocks.
Fear churned in every Persian.
We'd been led off the mark:
                            the Greeks
weren't running, no,
but sang that eerie triumph-chant
as men   640
        racing toward a fight
            and sure of winning.

Then the trumpet-shriek blazed
        through everything over there.
A signal:
        instantly
their oars struck salt.
                    We heard

that rhythmic rattle-slap.
It seemed no time till they   650
all stood in sight.
                We saw them sharp.
First the right wing,
    close-drawn, strictly ordered,
led out, and next we saw
the whole fleet bearing down, we heard
a huge voice
              Sons of Greece, go!
              Free fatherland,
              free children, wives,   660
              shrines of our fathers' gods,
              tombs where our forefathers lie.
              Fight for all we have!
              Now!
Then on our side shouts in Persian
rose to a crest.
                We didn't hold back.
That instant, ship rammed
bronzeclad beak on ship.
                It was   670
a Greek ship started the attack
shearing off a whole Phoenician
stern. Each captain steered his craft
    straight on one other.
At first the wave of Persia's fleet
rolled firm, but next, as our ships
    jammed into the narrows and
        no one could help any other and
            our own bronze teeth bit into
our own strakes,   680
        whole oarbanks shattered.
Then the Greek ships, seizing their chance,
swept in circling and struck and overturned
our hulls,
        and saltwater vanished before our eyes—
shipwrecks filled it, and drifting corpses.

Shores and reefs filled up with our dead
and every able ship under Persia's command
broke order,
     scrambling to escape.   690
We might have been tuna or netted fish,
for they kept on, spearing and gutting us
     with splintered oars and bits of wreckage,
while moaning and screams drowned out
the sea noise till
     Night's black face closed it all in.

Losses by thousands!
     Even if I told
the catalogue for ten full days I
could not complete it for you.   700
But this is sure:
     never before in one day
have so many thousands died.

ATOSSA It's true, then, true.
Wild seas of loss have come crashing down,
down over Persians and all Asia's tribes.

MESSENGER You must understand:
disaster—
     I've told you less than half.
The next load of suffering   710
outweighed the first twice over.

ATOSSA What more hateful Luck
could still beset our men?
     Answer me!
What fresh disaster, what
new losses weighted them down?

MESSENGER Persians at the peak of life,
     best in soul, brightest in lineage,
     first always to give the King loyalty—

they're dead without glory,   720
          and shamed by that fate.

ATOSSA (to the CHORUS)   Cruel chance!
O my friends, it hurts me.

                                        (to the MESSENGER)

How did they die? Can you say?

MESSENGER An island fronts the coast of Salamis—
          tiny, harborless,
                    where dance-wild
          Pan likes stepping it light through the breakers.
          There
                    Xerxes posted these chosen men,   730
          planning that when the shipwrecked enemy
          swam ashore desperate for safety,
          they'd kill that Greek force easily
          and rescue friends caught in the narrows.
          How badly he misread the future,
                    for after some god had
          handed Greeks the glory in the seafight,
          that same day
                    they fenced their bodies in bronze armor
          and leapt from their ships   740
                              and cordoned off
          the island so completely that our men milled
          helpless,
                    not knowing where to turn
          while stones battered at them
          and arrows twanging from the bowstrings
          hit home killing them.
                              It ended
          when the Greeks gave one great howl
          and charged, chopping meat   750
                    till every living man was butchered.

Then Xerxes moaned out loud
to see how deep disaster cut.
    Throned on a headland above the sea, he'd
    kept his whole army clear in sight.
And he ripped his clothes
and screamed
and gave shrill hasty shouts to his whole land force
dismissing them.
               They fled in disorder.   760

Here is disaster greater than the first
to make you groan.

ATOSSA (*looking up into the sky*)   You!
    Hateful, nameless, not human Power,
how You cheated Persians of their senses!
How bitter the vengeance
    meant for this talked-of Athens
that found its way home to my son!
Marathon killed men. Weren't they
enough?   770
    It was for them
my son cast retribution
and hauled in countless cruelties
    upon himself and us.

But the ships that outran doom—
    where did you leave them?
Do you know what happened?

MESSENGER The captains of the ships left
    ran in no order before the wind.
And the army left   780
    kept dropping off, first on Boiotian ground,
some of thirst,
    though water flowed beside them
      out of exhaustion's reach,
while some of us,

empty from panting,
drove through to the Phōkians' land
and Dōris' fields
and the Mēlian Gulf where
Sperkheios quenches the plain with earthkindly drink,   790
and after that Akhaian soil
and the cities of Thessaly took us in
when we were starving.
There the most died.
                    Thirst and hunger,
both of them stalked us.
And slogging north
on to Magnesia and on to Macedon,
we reached the Axios' ford
and Bolbē's reed-choked marsh   800
and Mt. Pangaios where Ēdōnians live.
It was that night
                some god
blew down winter out of season and froze
holy Strymōn bank to bank.
                    Then any man
who'd once thought gods were nothing
sought them out, praying, begging
as he lay face down before Earth and Sky.
When the army finished its godcalls,   810
it started to cross the icelocked water,
and those of us who step out quick
before the god can shed his rays
find ourselves safe,
but when the fireball of Sun came up,
blazing light and heat,
its flame melted the iceroad midstream
and men kept falling,
falling one on another, and he is lucky, yes,
whose life breath was quickest cut.   820

And those of us left to gain safety,
working through Thrace against hard odds,

have slipped away,
                    not many,
and come back to our homefires,
        to this earth of home.

Reason enough, chief city of Persians,
to cry out
        longing for your best belovèd youth.
True reasons, though there's much   830
I've left untold of horrors
that a god hurled
        crackling down on Persians.

                            The MESSENGER *exits right.*

CHORUS (*looking skyward*)   You!   Troublebringer!
        nameless and not human,
                how hard
You've jumped both feet into Persia's people!

ATOSSA I am heartsick. The army slaughtered!
        O vision in the night
                that roiled through dreams,   840
        the cruelties you clearly promised me
        came true.

(*to the* CHORUS)   And you,
you read them much too lightly.
Even so, there's only your advice
to seize and act on.
                            I will
first of all pray to the gods,
then bring gifts from my royal house—
        wine poured out with honey—   850
to soothe the appetites of Earth and ghosts.
When these are done, I shall
return to you.
                There's no regaining

what is gone, I understand that,
but I act so that something better
    may happen in days to come.

And you,
    with due regard for what has happened,
must, as my Faithful,   860
give advice worthy of my faith.

My son—
    if he comes back before I can return,
comfort him,
        escort him home
so that he heaps on existing evils
    no self-inflicted evil.

ATOSSA *remounts her chariot and exits right with her*
attendants.

CHORUS (chanting)   God, greatest King!
    The Persians' proud and manswollen army, now
You've destroyed it,   870
You've hidden
    Susa and Ekbatana in lowering grief

and mothers
    whose gentle hands savage their veils
    whose eyes rain tears on breasts already drenched
give tongue to sorrow

and wives, Persian brides
    wailing softly
    longing to see the men who were yokemates
    stripping the soft beds where bursting youth reveled   880
wail, wail out the hungriest grief

And I, too,
    raise a griefswollen voice

at the fate of men gone
dead and gone

(*singing and dancing*)

Listen   To the outmost ends
       Asia's earth groans now
              emptied of sons
Xerxes   convoyed them
                            He   CONVOYED THEM   890
Xerxes   destroyed them
                            He   DESTROYED THEM
Xerxes   the hothead brought on the whole rout
       he and his riverdhows rigged for the sea

              Once
                     we knew Darius' rule
                     a bowchief who
                     never volleyed such hurt
                     and Susa's men loved him
              WHY HAVE TIMES CHANGED?   900

Soldiers and seamen lost!
       Sailwings unfurled, bluedark
              eyes on the sea
warships   convoyed them
                            Ships   CONVOYED THEM
warships   destroyed them
                            Ships   DESTROYED THEM
warships
              brought every one of them down
       rammed them and left them to Greeks' hacking   910
              hands

              Now
                     we learn the King himself
                     by slender chance
                     runs for life down snowblocked

roads in sweeping Thrace
HOW CAN THIS BE?

Those doomed to die first
DOOMED
are left
there was no choice   920
LEFT
to wash on Salamis' wavebroken rocks
THEY ARE GONE
Groan
Bite lips till the blood shows
Howl, griefweighted voices, howl
anguish at heaven
DEAD AND GONE
Hold sorrow's burden
till breath sobs and breaks   930

Flesh torn in the surge
TORN
is stripped
clean off the bone
STRIPPED
by voiceless young of the unsoilable Sea
THEY ARE GONE
Grieve
you houses robbed of your men
Wail, childless parents, wail   940
inhuman anguish
DEAD AND GONE
and learn in your grey years
the whole reach of pain

And those who live on Asia's broad earth
will not long be ruled
by Persian law
nor longer pay tribute
under empire's commanding grip

67

nor fling themselves earthward   950
    in awe of kingship
        whose strength now lies dead

No longer will tongues in vassal mouths
be kept under guard
                for people are freed,
set loose to bark freedom
now that dominion's yoke is snapped
The bloodsodden beaches
    of Ajax' sea-bruised island
        now hold Persia's heart   960

ATOSSA, *on foot and dressed in mourning, enters right
with her ladies, who carry the jars and garlands needed
for making libations.*

ATOSSA (*speaking in iambic verse*) Good friends,
        whoever lives learns by experience
    that when a wave of evils crests
    and breaks, it's natural for humankind
        to be afraid of everything,
    but when the deathless Power flows calm,
        to trust
    that Fortune's wind will always blow fair.
    But now, for me,
        everything is packed with fear,   970
    before my eyes the gods' hostility shows plain,
    and the roar in my ears is battle din,
        not a healing song:
    Evils attack so fiercely panic storms my heart.

That's the reason I've returned
        without a chariot or queenly luxury
    to bring my son's father the appeasing drinks
        that serve as sweeteners to dead men:

            (*pointing to the jars her ladies carry*)

an unblemished Cow's white freshtasting milk
and the Flowerworker's droplets, lightsteeped honey,   980
with moisture poured sparkling from a virgin Spring
and unwatered drink from a wild country mother—
     this, the ancient Vine's new brightness,
and the fresh-scented harvest of one who blooms life
always in her leaves, the sundrenched Olive Tree—
     here it is,
and woven flowers, children of Allbearing Earth.

But, O my friends,
     these libations to the ones below
need solemn hymns.   990
               Chant them
and call his spirit, call up Darius
     while I send down
these Earthdrunk honors to the gods below.

CHORUSLEADER (*chanting*) Our Queen, our lady,
          whom Persians revere,
     yes,
          send your libations to Earth's hidden rooms
     while we, chanting, calling, pour out our breath
     to beg kindness from those who marshal   1000
          men's shadows through Earth.

ATOSSA *and her ladies make their ceremonies of libation,
while the* CHORUS *look on with increasing anxiety. When
she has finished, they begin the ghostraising.* ATOSSA,
weeping, muffled, sits at the tomb's base.

CHORUS (*chanting*) Help us, You Powers undying and holy
          that thrive beneath graves.
     You, Earth and the Soul-Guide
     and You who are King of the dead below us,
     send him out of his utter darkness,
          send his spirit up into light.

69

Disasters keep stalking us,
                    and if
he knows of any cure   1010
          more powerful than offerings and prayer,
only risen near us into light
          can he reveal it.

                              (singing and dancing)

Can he hear me?
          Blest in death
                    and potent as a deathless Force
can my King hear these broken words
          earthmuffled
                    tumbling from my lips and touching
                              every note of pain in   1020
ceaseless sorrow-roughened breath?
Or must I shout
          so that my anguish reaches him?
Can he heed me in his buried dark?

Wake and hear me
          Earth and You
                    Who rule that world where dead men go
Give complete consent to prayer:
          set free
                    his proud and deathless glory   1030
                              Let Persia's god, born a man in Susa
rise now from his funeral house
Now, speed him up
          whose peer does not nor ever shall
rest hidden in this Persian earth

Man I loved, yes
          tomb I love, for
everything I love lies covered there
Hand of Death
          Yours alone the power to open graves   1040

and lead him lightward
                    Hand of Death
          free our hallowed lord Darius
Free him

Never once
          did he kill men with
Folly's blind and life-devouring haste
He was
          called the Persians' godbright counselor
and godbright counselor   1050
                              he was
          who steered the army on a true course.
Free him

The CHORUS *fall to their knees and begin to hammer and
claw at the earth as if to help free the* GHOST OF DARIUS.
            In their next words they invoke him directly.

Shah once and Shah forever
          come close
               break through
Go to the high prow of your tomb
Make yourself known
          showing signs of your kingship
               crocus-dyed shoe   1060
               turban's upright crest
Make yourself seen
                    Break free
Father who brought us no evil
Darius
          break free

Wake and hear loud suffering
          Hear strange
               new pain
Lord of our lord, find daylight form   1070
The deathmist

that grows on the eyes of the dying
opens dark wings:
the young men, our sons
are all of them gone
Wake now
Father who brought us no evil
Darius
awake

The CHORUS, moaning, slowly stand.

CHORUSLEADER Why, why   1080
must friends who deeply mourned your death
[now mourn again—
sorrows twice borne, new grief exciting old?]
Where have we erred?
The fleet all Asia built
is smashed and sunk,
the three-tiered
ships
ghostships ghostships.

The GHOST OF DARIUS rises, spectral, from his tomb.

DARIUS (speaking in iambic verse) Most Faithful of the faithful,   1090
comrades of my youth,
Persians grown honorably grey,
what trouble oppresses my people?
The earth ceiling groans—
hammered, scratched open.

(to ATOSSA)

And seeing you, who shared my bed, here
huddled now beside my tomb,
I sense fear.
Yes,
I drank the sweetenings that you poured down.   1100

(*to the* CHORUS)

And you who stand before my tomb
wail dirges
and dolefully chant out soulraising spells
to summon me.
There is no easy exit:
Gods in the underrealms have always been
better at taking than letting go.
Yet, now that I am one of them and powerful,
I come.
Be quick, for I would have   1110
no blame for moments spent beneath the sun.
What new strange evils
weigh down my Persians?

ATOSSA *sobs. The* CHORUS *prostrate themselves.*

CHORUS (*singing*) I praise you
and awe blinds my eyes
I praise you
but awe binds my tongue
Your nearness fills me
with death's age-old chill

DARIUS (*speaking in trochaic verse*)
Because you chanted spells   1120
persuading me to leave the buried world,
I come.
Tell everything, not rambling on,
but make the story brief.
Speak and be done.
I frighten you?
Then reverence exceeds its bounds.
Let reverence go.

CHORUS (*singing*) I dread you
and would not displease   1130

I dread you
        but cannot find speech
to tell those I love
        news better left untold

ATOSSA *laments.* (DARIUS *and* ATOSSA *speak in trochaic*
                                verse from here through line 1254.)

DARIUS Because you feel the old dread
                pounding in your hearts,
                        restraining you,
        then let the one
                who shared my bed,
                        my aged lady wife,   1140
        cease her lamenting
                to give me
                        plain account.
        Mankind is
                bound to suffer
                        the hurts of being human.
        Many the evils spawned in the sea
                and many on land
                        for you who must die.
        And the longer you live,   1150
                the greater
                        your pain.

ATOSSA My husband, you
                above all other men were destined
                        to a wealth of happiness.
        How fortunate you were!
                While your living eyes
                        beheld the sun,
        Persians,
                filled with praise and envy,   1160
                        called you a god.
        Now do I envy you
                because you died

before you looked in the depths of loss.
Listen, Darius,
    I need few words
        to tell you everything:
Persia's power,
    her prosperity
        are completely crushed.   1170

DARIUS How? Thunderbolts of plague? Civil war?

ATOSSA Neither. Near Athens the whole expedition was lost.

DARIUS Which of my sons invaded Greece?

ATOSSA Headstrong Xerxes. He emptied Asia.

DARIUS Stubborn child! Did he go by land or sea?

ATOSSA Both. With a double front of two contingents.

DARIUS But how could footsoldiers cross the sea?

ATOSSA He made a path by yoking the Hellespont.

DARIUS What? He closed mighty Bosporos?

ATOSSA Yes. I think Something divine gave him help.   1180

DARIUS Something so monstrous it twisted his good sense!

ATOSSA And we see his achievement—disaster.

DARIUS What happened? Why do you groan?

ATOSSA Because the ships sank, the army was lost.

DARIUS You mean the whole army fell to the spear?

ATOSSA And Susa's man-empty streets are groaning.

DARIUS Lost, a great army! Our defense, lost!

ATOSSA And Bactria's men, even the old ones, are all dead.

DARIUS Wretched man! He killed his allies' young sons.

ATOSSA But Xerxes—it's said that he and a few others—   1190

DARIUS Is he safe?

ATOSSA —happily did reach the bridge yoking two shores.

DARIUS And arrived safe in Asia? You're sure?

ATOSSA Yes, it's been clearly reported. There is no doubt.

DARIUS Too swiftly then
                the Oracles came true,
                        and on my son
        Zeus hurled down
                prophecy completed,
                        and I had somehow   1200
        hoped that gods
                would take a longer time
                        to work their plan.
        But when a man
                speeds toward his own ruin,
                        a god gives him help.
        Now a fountain of defeats
                has been struck
                        for everyone I love.
        And my son in his ignorance,   1210
                his reckless youth,
                        brought on its spurt:
        he hoped to dam
                the flow of holy Hellespont—
                        the Bosporos

that streams from god—
    by locking it
        in shackles like a slave
and he altered the strait
    and, casting over it   1220
        hammered chains,
made a footpath
    broad enough
        for his broad array of troops.
Mere man that he is,
    he thought, but not on good advice,
        he'd overrule all gods,
Poseidon most of all.
    How can this not be
        a sickness of mind   1230
that held my son?
    The wealth
        I earned by my own hard work
may be overturned,
    becoming nothing more than
        spoils to the first looting hand.

ATOSSA   Consort with evil-minded men
            taught headstrong Xerxes
                what to think:
        they told him   1240
            that the vast wealth
                you handed on
        was won at spearpoint
            while he,
                not half the man,
        secretly played toy spears at home
            and added nothing
                to inherited prosperity.
        Hearing such taunts
            over and again   1250
                from evil-minded men,
        he planned

his expedition
and the invasion of Greece.

(ALL *speak in iambic verse from here till the end of the*
episode.)

DARIUS And so did his work,
the greatest ever,
to be remembered always,
such work as never before fell
and emptied out Susa
since the Lord Zeus granted this honor: 1260
that one man
should rule vast sheepbreeding Asia,
his sceptre held
as a steersman holds the rudder.
The Mede himself was the army's first leader,
and another, his son, gained the succession
because reason stood at his passions' helm,
and third after him Cyrus ruled,
Heaven's favorite,
who gave peace to everyone he loved   1270
and made subject Lydia's people and Phrygia's
and rounded up all Asian Greeks by force
nor did the god despise him,
for his heart was righteous,
and Cyrus' son, fourth, piloted the army,
and fifth Mardos led, a disgrace to fatherland
and long-established throne,
but there was plotting
and Artaphrenes, potent in virtue,
helped by friends whose duty it was,   1280
cut him down inside the palace.
Then I ruled.
Chosen by lot, I gained what I wished for
and fought a thousand times with my fighting thousands
but never
threw evil like this on the nation.

But Xerxes my son, green in years,
    thinks green
and forgets what I taught him.

                     (*to the* CHORUS)

But you, men of my own generation,   1290
    plainly understand
that everyone of us who has held power
cannot be shown
    to have worked such devastation.

CHORUS What next, lord Darius?
    Where will your prophecy attain
its end? How, after the worst,
may we, Persia's people, win through to the best?

DARIUS Beware: mount no soldiers against Greek holdings.
Beware: not even if Medes count more soldiers.   1300
Know: Earth Herself is their ally.

CHORUS What do you mean? How, their ally?

DARIUS She starves a manglutted enemy.

CHORUS But you must know
    we shall select choice, action-ready troops.

DARIUS But you must learn
    the army still remaining on Greek soil
shall not see a day of safe return.

CHORUS What are you saying?
    That not all the forces left   1310
will cross the Hellespont from Europe?

DARIUS Few out of thousands,
    if one can trust godspoken oracles.

But when you look at those that have come true,
you know they are fulfilled—
    complete, not just in part.
And if this be so, then
    empty hopes have persuaded him
to leave behind a force selected from the army,
and there they linger   1320
    where Asōpos pours kind floods on Boiotia's soil:
for them the height of evil waits implacable
to pay them back in suffering
    for pride and godlessness
who came to Greek earth lacking the reverence
    to stay their hands
from desecrating gods' images
    and putting temples to the torch,
and altars are vanished
    and shrines dedicated to the undying   1330
Dead are torn, root and branch, from their bases
    and shattered.
It is sure
    that having done evil, no less
do they suffer and more in the future
and not yet has evil's wellspring run dry
    but still spurts unchecked:
so great shall be new
    sacrifices of clotting blood
poured out   1340
    on Plataia's battleground by Dorian spears,
so great the piles of bones,
even to the third generation they shall be
seen by human eyes as speechless warnings
that those who must die
    not overreach themselves::
when stubborn pride has flowered, it
ripens to self-deception
    and the only harvest is a glut of tears.

            (directly to the CHORUS)

These are the punishments   1350
      and as you behold them,
remember Athens and remember Greece
      lest someone
scorning the immediate blessings Heaven grants,
lusting for others,
      pour away his worldly goods and happiness.
Zeus the Pruning Shear of arrogance run wild
is set over you, a grim accountant.
Because events have prophesied
      that my son learn to know himself,   1360
teach him in gentle admonitions
to stop
      wounding gods with young reckless pride.

                                        (to ATOSSA)

And you,
      agèd mother whom Xerxes loves,
after you have gone to your house
      and found him splendor that suits a king,
go out to face your son
whose anguish at the fullness of disaster
has torn his bright embroideries   1370
      to shredded rags around his body.
But speak kind words in a calming voice.
He will listen only to you
      and only you can comfort him.

DARIUS begins to descend into the tomb, his voice fading.

I go, I must,
down below earth to the shadowworld.
Goodbye, wise old friends.
Though evil surrounds you,
give joy to your souls
all the days that you live   1380
for wealth is

                    useless to
                        the dead

                                        DARIUS *vanishes.*

CHORUSLEADER Disasters present and disasters coming on—
                    I listened with anguish
                        to the Asians' fate.

        ATOSSA (*looking skyward*) You! Nameless, inhuman!
                    How cruel the anguish
                invading me! And one disaster
                    most of all bites deep—   1390
                to hear that shame's clothing
                    hangs in ragged shreds around my son's body.

                                            (*to the* CHORUS)

        But I'm going home, and when I've taken
                kingly splendor from my house,
        I'll try to face him.
        Though evil surrounds us,
                I shall not forsake my best belovèd son.

                            With her ladies ATOSSA *exits right.*

    CHORUS (*singing and dancing*)   GOD, PITY US
                for once we knew
            the life of grandeur and virtue   1400
                    under stable rule
            when he whose years and dignity we honored—
            the All-Enabler, the Evil-Shunner,
            the Battle-Winner—
                            when King
            Darius cast a god's light
                and governed us wholly

        AND PITY US
                for once we showed

an armed force whose praises rang sharp   1410
        through the chastened world
The laws that steered us stood bold on towers
and days of return led men safely home
Unwearied, unwounded,
                    the men
of Persia came back from war
        to houses that prospered

How many cities he captured
        without once crossing the Halys river
        nor leaving his hearth: 1420
city on city—
        the Rivergod's cities
                piled on the floodplain near Strymōn's gulf
and hillguarded cattletowns in Thrace

and cities east of the coastal marshes—
        tower-enclosed mainland cities
        bowed to him as lord,
and boastful cities
        by Hellē's broad current
                and strung on the shores of the Inland Sea   1430
and cities clustered at the Black Sea's mouth

And wave-caressed islands
        held in the Sea's arm
                close off our homeshores:
Lesbos
and olive-silvery Samos
Khios
and Paros
Naxos
Mykonos   1440
Tenos, too
        that rises out of the deep near
Andros

and salt-embraced islands
   set in the Sea's midst—
      he mastered them, too:
Lemnos
and Ikaros' settling place
Rhodes, Knidos
and Cypriote cities—   1450
Paphos
and Soloi
Salamis, too
   whose mother-city now causes
our groans

And more,
that rich estate Ionia
   teeming with Greeks—
he bent it to his will
and drew on strength that never failed: 1460
     fighters under heavy arms
     allies from a thousand tribes

But now
   beyond a doubt
we must endure
being god-overturned in war,
for we are tamed
   greatly tamed
     by seastruck blows

XERXES *enters left hidden from view in a curtained
carriage drawn by ragged men. A few other survivors
straggle in, pulling worn equipment carts.*

XERXES (*chanting*) No!   1470
       Nonono!
Heartsick have I confronted hateful doom.
No warning signs, not one, foretold me
some undying Lust for human flesh

would stamp savagely on Persia's clans.
What now?
                    I am helpless,
my body's last current of strength runs out
and I must
                    face townfathers, fathers of sons.   1480

Dear God!
                    Would that I were with the men
now gone. I wish
the doom of death had curtained me.

CHORUSLEADER (chanting)   My King,
devote your sorrow to the skillful thousands,
the sweeping primacy of Persia's rule,
and the straight rows of men
          some deathless Power cut flat.

CHORUS (rising from chant into full song)
And Earth herself   1490
          mourns. Listen! She cries out
wailing her own young   slaughtered by Xerxes
who crammed them into the huge maw of Death,
          for those now dead
were thousands of men
                              the country's flower
tamers of great bows   thickets of men
all wasted and withered
          by tens of thousands.
Cry! Can you cry?   1500
                    Their courage kept us safe.
And Asia
          whose mountains and plains you rule
is forced   forced in blood
          down on her knees.

XERXES, dressed in rags, climbs from the carriage. Both
he and the CHORUS sing from this point until the end.

XERXES Look at me
            and weep
                I am
            your sorrow, a sad hollow
            son to Earth and my fathers   1510
                    born to bring home woe

CHORUS There are greetings for your safe return:
            bleak howls of woe
            bleak melodies of woe
                torn from the throats of
                    dirge-keening men
            I promise you
                promise you
                    tear-darkened notes

XERXES Let every breath   1520
            you draw
                sound out
            a din of endless lamenting
            Divine wind has shifted   Heaven
                    blows against me now

CHORUS Every breath drawn shall din a lament
            sounding your pain
            and sea-battered sorrows
                But listen! a nation
                    howls for her children   1530
            And I ring
                I ring out
                    a tear-spilling change

XERXES It was Greeks
                who stole our victory!
            Yes, Greeks
                for whom ship-armored War
                    decided
            to harvest

86

the black as night plain
and that Luck-hated shore

CHORUS Thousands
the thousands!
Anguish puts questions:
Where are the friends
who marched legion behind you?
Where, the men
who stood proud beside you?
Where, Pharandakes?
Where are Sousas, Pelagon, Dotamas?   1550
Where, Agdabatas, Psammis, too
and where Sousiskanes
who left Ekbatana?

WHERE ARE THEY NOW?

XERXES Past all help
I *had* to leave them
They fell
from a Tyrian ship
and washed on
Salamis'   1560
rocks and there they died
on that wave-broken shore

CHORUS Thousands
the thousands!
Where are the others?
Where, your Pharnoukhos
and Ariomardos?
Where is his brave heart?
And where, lord Seualkes
or highborn Lilaios?   1570
Where are Memphis, Tharybis, Masistras?
Where, Artembares, Hystaikhmas, too?
We ask you, keep asking you
over and over

WHERE ARE THEY NOW?

XERXES Sorrow

    sorrow

        is mine, mine

Looking with one same look at

    Athens   old as time, anciently hated   1580

all of them now   at one same sweeping stroke

are cast on the dry land

to lie there

        lie there

    gasping for breath

CHORUS Then it's true?

        Your most faithful Persian

your very own Eye

    whose rollcall counted those thousands

TEN thousands—   1590

Batanokhos' son Alpistos

    [you left HIM there]

with the son of Sesames, Megabates' son?

Parthos, too, and brawny Oibares?

You left them all

        left them

slaughtered or drowned?

      To Persia's old men you

call out a roll

    of grief, unbounded grief   1600

XERXES Sorrow

    sorrow

      If only I

could charm back the souls of

    brave men   comrades you make me remember

as you call   the roll of boundless grief

hateful, unforgettable grief

My heart howls

        howls

    from its bony cage   1610

CHORUS And I ache
                with longing for others:
          Xanthes who led out
                ten thousand nomads
          and war-hungry Ankhares, too
          Diaixis with another, Arsakes
                horselords both of them
          and Ēgdadatas and more, Lythimnas
          Tolmos, too, whose spear always thirsted
          I am stunned   1620
                stunned
          They'll not march again
                beside these men, these few
          who came home
                following your carriage wheels

XERXES Gone, the leaders who set my army's pace

CHORUS   Gone, gone, their names become dust

XERXES Ache   aching sorrow

CHORUS   Sorrow sorrow
                     Undying Powers   1630
           You willed this hopeless loss
                wide and chilling as Blind Folly's gaze

XERXES Struck, we are struck lifelong by Luck's blows

CHORUS   Struck, struck down, I know it to the bone

XERXES By new   strange new anguish

CHORUS   From the moment
                     Greek sailors
           loomed on fortune's horizon
           War-broken   no, not Persia's sons!

XERXES How not?   1640

Thousands lost—
struck through my army   I suffer

CHORUS   Great fool!
                    What is NOT
              ruined   that made Persia proud?

XERXES   (*fingering his rags*)   Do you see the remnant left as my
              cover?

CHORUS   I see, I do see!

XERXES   (*holding up his quiver*)   And see this arrow-concealing—

CHORUS   You're telling us something is saved!

XERXES   —this storehouse where shafts were crowded?   1650

CHORUS   Few left of many, too few

XERXES   Defenders are few, we are helpless

CHORUS   Greeks never ran from the spear

XERXES   War-mad,
                    they made me
              see shame   I never expected—

CHORUS   You speak
                    of DEFEAT!
              Ship-armored thousands   went down

XERXES   —and I tore my clothes when I saw them drowning   1660

CHORUS   Despair despair

XERXES   Far more than despair

CHORUS   Disasters by twos, disasters by threes

XERXES In my shame I give joy to our enemies

CHORUS And strength is wholly destroyed

XERXES My bodyguard's gone, I am naked

CHORUS Stripped of friends, tricked at sea

XERXES Wail tearsongs, wail pain, wail me home

CHORUS Gone, gone, they are gone, dead and gone

XERXES Din back my howling, my thumping   1670

CHORUS Sad voices sadly moan sadness

XERXES Cry doomsongs, tune them to mine

CHORUS Gone   gone
&   dead and gone
XERXES   gone

CHORUS How brutal the losses on land and sea
How helpless my grief

XERXES Strike deathnotes, drum breasts, drum me home

CHORUS Dead, dead, they are dead and I weep

XERXES Din back my howling, my thumping   1680

CHORUS Lead and I follow, my lord

XERXES Lift voices, beat out the dirge

CHORUS Gone   gone
&   dead and gone
XERXES   gone

CHORUS And black-bruising hands and voice bruised black
        now mingle in grief

XERXES And keep striking breasts and keep crooning wails

CHORUS   Wail thousands the thousands

XERXES And tug, pull out white hair from your beards   1690

CHORUS   With tearing, tearing nails and a dirge

XERXES And rake air with cries

CHORUS   Hear my cries

XERXES And rip heavy robes with fingers hooked

CHORUS   Mourn thousands the thousands

XERXES And strip out your hair, lament an army lost

CHORUS   With tearing, tearing nails and a dirge

XERXES And eyes rain down tears

CHORUS   See my tears

XERXES Din back my howling, my thumping   1700

CHORUS   Thousands the thousands

XERXES Lament as you go to your houses

CHORUS   Sorrow the sorrow
            Hard now to tread Persia's downtrodden Earth

XERXES Wail as you step through the city

CHORUS   Wailing wails, weeping

XERXES Tread soft as you sob out your dirges

CHORUS   Sorrow our sorrow
                  Hard now to tread Persia's downtrodden Earth

XERXES Mourn mourn   1710
              the men in the ships   three-tiered ships
          Mourn mourn
              your sons dead and gone   dead and gone

CHORUS To slowdinning dirges we shall lead you home

          The CHORUS surround XERXES. Together, lamenting and
          making all the gestures of mourning, they circle the stage
                          as if walking through the city.

                          Exeunt ALL right.

NOTES AND GLOSSARY

NOTES

1-182 During this long passage, which occupies more than one-eighth of the total running time, the Chorus alone carry the play—are the play. Although the effects produced are both varied and, in a certain sense, highly dramatic, they are brought about by costume, movement, and rhythm, not by any interplay between separate characters on the stage. This is Aeschylean poetic drama at its most remote from our modern theatrical experience; here, therefore, the visual and aural imagination, whether of the reader or of the director, must work at its hardest.

In Greek theatrical terminology (see on 183-867) the whole passage is called the *parodos*, the "side-entrance" of the Chorus. In the Greek, 1-90 are in the anapestic marching rhythm; here we are to imagine the Chorus as entering from one of the side-passages (also called *parodos*), and chanting as they move around the orchestra, their movement perhaps reinforcing the onward-marching effect produced by the great roll-call of the imperial forces which is the predominant content of the chant. In 91-182 the metre shows that they are no longer chanting but singing; dance and mime will now replace the marching. The singing in turn falls into three parts: 91-136, 137-48 (see also the separate note on those lines), and 149-82. The first two parts are composed in the same song-metre, the Ionic (basically $\cup \cup - -$), a rhythm which heaves like the sea's swell. In 91-136 we hear of the still unclouded majesty of the expedition, and of its invincible progress, but at 137-48 those thoughts are suddenly interrupted—still in the same metre!—by a meditation on the deceptiveness of God, and on the man-trap set by Ātē. This leads, at 149, to a violent change in the metre and presumably also in the character of the dance. From here until the song's end at 182, the Chorus mourn for a land imagined as empty of its menfolk. The iambo-trochaic rhythm which predominates here has been thought by some students to derive originally from Greek funeral laments; however that may be, it will certainly recur, loud and clear, in the Greek of the play's finale, from 1626 until the end. Thus, it will be seen, almost all the varied emotions of this play, and its arc of triumph and disaster, have been foreshadowed by the Chorus before a single actor has set foot in the theater.

17-18 *and now . . . King's name* We offer a guess at the meaning underlying the Greek here, which seems almost certainly corrupt; as it stands, it seems to say "and yaps young man!"

28-44 *You, Amistres . . . and you* The Greek is in the third person throughout this passage. The word "you" is used in our version to capture the effect of the repetitive *kai* and *te . . . te* ("and," "both . . . and") which link the names in the Greek.

91-92 *Persians, Breakers-of-cities* By a strange fatality of language, the word *persai* means in Greek both "Persians" and "to destroy," and more than once Aeschylus seems to play on this ambiguity. Our words attempt to translate the heavy compound adjective, *perse-ptolis*, which he applies to the invasion-force here; the second part of it, *ptolis*, means "city."

106 *gold-showered line* The Greek text, on the most commonly accepted reading, says, literally, "born-of-gold line." Aeschylus probably alludes here to a Greek belief which is recorded by Herodotus (VII.61 and 150) and by some later writers: that the Persians are so named because they trace their descent from one Perses, a son of that great Greek hero Perseus who was begotten by Zeus upon Danae in a shower of gold.

137-48 *But how crafty . . . escape unhurt* The metre and reading of this passage, as it appears in the manuscripts, present many difficulties in detail, but there is no doubt as to the general sense. It is a sudden and frightful intuition of the fragility of human greatness in face of the Divine, and of the vast power of "Blind Folly" (for which the Greek is *Ātē*). For the present, this remains mere intuition; only much later in the play, with the epiphany of Darius' Ghost, will its true application to the Persian expedition be made clear. A very difficult question, which has been debated for a century and a half with plausible arguments on either side and yet still without a generally agreed solution, is, where should this passage stand? In all the manuscripts it appears *before* the lines which we number 123-36 ("For gods decree . . . they stride the waves"). It was a nineteenth-century German scholar, Karl Otfried Müller, who first argued that its original position must have been *after* those lines, so that it would provide at once a sinister coda to the climactic passage on the Persians' achievements, and a natural transition to the wild lamentation which sets in at 149. After much pondering of the arguments, we have come down on the side of Müller; but we do not pretend to certainty here.

183-867 This is the first episode, according to the terminology which has been used to describe the formal, metrical-musical articulation of a Greek tragedy since at least the time of Aristotle (*Poetics*, chapter XII, where an *episode* is defined as that part of a tragedy that "lies between complete choral songs"). As has been seen in the Introduction, p. 25, n. 31, these formal divisions do not necessarily coincide with the main phases in the dramatic development of our play. This particular *episode* is, in fact, unusually rich and complex both in its content and in its metrical effects. So far as content goes, a decisive break occurs at the first speech of the Messenger in 417-25 (on which see the Introduction, pp. 23–25). Before that, we have felt only vague apprehensions about the vulnerability of the Persian host to the operation of divine law; after it, the truth of the calamity is certain, and its details are spelled out in the long narrative speeches of the Messenger. Metrically, Aeschylus' Greek moves through all three of the levels of utterance available to a Greek tragedian: unaccompanied speech, chant, and full song (see the Introduction, p. 20). He further uses the metre called the trochaic tetrameter (on which see 201, note). These shifts in metre are indicated, as usual, in our marginal notes, and it will be observed how closely they follow, as it were, the contours of the *episode*'s content: chant to accompany the physical movements at the opening, trochaics for the flustered dialogues between Chorus and Queen, steady iambic speech for prolonged exposition, and bursts of full song to bring out the Chorus' horror as the news strikes home.

184 *this ancient roof* See the Introduction, pp. 18–19.

189 *son of Darius* After these words the Greek manuscripts offer a mysterious phrase, apparently to be translated "related to us in virtue of his father's name." Following most modern editors, we have omitted it; it looks like a fragment of some ancient Greek reader's marginal comment, mistakenly copied into the poetic text.

194 *Look up* The stage-direction before this line is based on 975-76, where the Queen, on re-entering, says that she comes this time "without a chariot or queenly luxury." Following an editorial tradition which goes back through the medieval manuscripts of Aeschylus to the Alexandrian scholars, we have named the queen ATOSSA in our *Dramatis Personae*, our stage-directions, and often elsewhere. Modern scholars have pointed out that that name never, in fact, occurs in the verse-text of the *Persians*, and have deduced that Aeschylus (either for dramatic reasons or because he actually did not know much about the historical Atossa) did not care to particularize; all he intended his audience to see here was a nameless Oriental Queen-Mother. This deduction is almost certainly correct, and is worth bearing in mind when one comes finally to assess the play in its aspect as a historical document. On the other hand, the point did not seem important enough to justify the inconvenience which would result if we broke with the age-old convention which is still retained in most of the major editions. See further in the Glossary, under ATOSSA.

201 *My lady* From here to 269 the Chorus and the Queen converse in the metre called the trochaic tetrameter. The *Persians* contains two other dialogue-passages composed in this metre: 346-415 in the present episode, and 1120-1254 (with the exception of the lyric passage at 1129-34) in the Darius episode. In Greek it is a long and agitated verse-line—a fairly close English analogue to it is Browning's line in *Home-Thoughts from the Sea*, "Nobly, nobly Cape Saint Vincent to the North-West died away"—and not too easy, one would imagine, for an actor to sustain at any length. In this translation it has been handled for the most part by short triplets, each beginning and ending with an accented syllable.

According to chapter IV of Aristotle's *Poetics*, the trochaic tetrameter was the prime dialogue-metre of the very earliest Attic tragedy, being replaced only after some time by the more natural and more easily speakable iambic trimeter. The presence of so many trochaic tetrameters in this, the earliest tragedy to survive, may perhaps be a vestige of that earliest phase of the art. Aeschylus never uses them on anything like this scale again in his extant plays; nor does Sophocles; only Euripides, in the plays composed at the very end of his career, reintroduces them for long dialogue-scenes, apparently as a deliberate archaism and to enhance the operatic quality which he aimed at in his latest work. Opinions vary as to whether they were delivered as recitative with instrumental accompaniment (like the anapests), or unaccompanied (like the iambic trimeters). For practical production purposes, we have assumed the latter in our stage-directions.

203 *sonbearing*   The Greek word is *bathyzōnōn*, deep-girdled or -belted. The word has been re-imagined here as referring to more than a woman's mode of dress. It seems to suggest the set of a belt on hips and the deep roundness of a pelvis that gives easy passage to children: Persia's mothering-lifegiving-sonbearing women. And Atossa, for mothering a king, is most honored among them. Pindar uses the same word to describe the Graces, goddesses of fertility and increase, in his ninth Pythian ode, lines 2-3.

211 *Lust for Winning*   The Greek has *daimon*.

221-45 *It's you . . . bodies' strength*   The text and meaning of these lines are much debated; particularly problematic are the details of the tremendous image of personified Wealth (*ploutos*) in 228-33, and the syntax of 238-45, both of which are confused in the Greek text presented by the manuscripts. To us, it does not seem beyond the bounds of possibility that that text is actually what Aeschylus composed, the hectic quality of the trochaic metre being quite deliberately matched by a certain stylistic confusion in order to bring out the tumult of the Queen's emotions as the scene opens. But in any case, the general drift of her words is certain: like the Chorus in their preceding song, she is assailed by thoughts of the fragility of success.

275 *bent on making it Persian and his*   The Greek says, literally, "wishing to *persai* it"; for the pun, see 91-92, note.

278 kind-hearted dark This translates a single word, euphronē, which the tragedians sometimes use for "night"; literally "kind-heart" or "glad-
heart," it seems to derive from some primeval desire to propitiate
the dark time, the time of dreams, by speaking well of it. The
same word is used below, 366.

291 the great world beyond The Greek has "the barbaros earth." This is the first
of ten occurrences of the word barbaros in this play, mostly with
reference to the Persians. We have paraphrased it on each occasion, because the English derivative words "barbarian," "barbaric,"
with their evil nuances, are clearly ruled out. Barbaros originally
had a neutral meaning: "non-Greek" in speech, race, or location;
and although the fatal dichotomy between Greek (or Western)
"civilization" and non-Greek "barbarism" was beginning to open
up in the course of the fifth century, it is scarcely perceptible in
this play. Those critics who, at least in the past, have represented
the Persians (especially its finale) as a kind of mocking triumph
over a silly and alien race, might have given more thought to this
very passage: in the dream, Persia and Greece are seen as sisters,
both of marvelous majesty and beauty (284-88; and compare 106,
note).

321 to cleanse me of bad dreams Not in the Greek; we have included the words
because to a modern reader the reason for the Queen's recourse
to spring water will probably not be so self-evident as it would
have been to the first audience.

323 Phoibos' altar This is perhaps the most striking of the occasional appearances
of Greek gods in this Persian setting (on which see the Introduction, p. 21, note 30). It has been argued, unprovably but plau-
sibly, that Aeschylus may have had some knowledge of the religious practices of the Persians; and that what we have in this
passage is a perfectly realistic fire-altar of Ahuramazda, with
merely a change in the God's name as a concession to the Athenian audience. Phoibos, "Shining One," is of course an often-used
epithet of Apollo.

324 mixed honey and wine The Greek for this is pelanos; see 1339, note.

343 his people cannot call him to account The Greek says, literally, "he is not
accountable, hypeuthynos, to the city." Here Aeschylus uses

terms which are really applicable only to a Greek democratic city-state, not to the Persian monarchy. There can be no doubt that he is stressing what to a Greek (and most notably to Herodotus, a generation later) was one of the most important issues in the struggle between Greek and Persian: it was not merely a clash between nations, but also a clash between political systems; and it was the democratic system that won, against all odds. *Hypeuthynos*, in particular, stands out as an Athenian democratic technical term, referring to the *euthynē*, the public accounting, which every elected magistrate was bound to undergo at the end of his annual term of office. It is surely no accident that much later in the play a similar term will occur in the Greek: Darius' ghost, in 1358, will explain that over the proud thoughts which resulted in the disaster of Plataia there stands as corrector "Zeus, a grim accountant, *euthynos*." In the end, it will prove, even a Shah must undergo his *euthynē* . . . but before God.

401-5 *Such that . . . in their soil* There is much debate as to the reading, the meaning, and even the order of these lines. Doubtfully, we have accepted the line-order and interpretations offered in Broadhead's edition. In spite of these uncertainties, the historical allusions in the lines are clear enough. 401 will refer to the Athenian repulse of the Persians at Marathon (see the Glossary under that name), and perhaps also to the Athenian part in a raid on the Persian provincial capital at Sardis in ca. 498 B.C. (described in Herodotus, V.99-102 and 105); 405, the "fountain of silver," must refer to the recent opening-up of exceptionally large veins of silver ore in the Attic mines at Laureion (Herodotus, VII.144).

409 *So well . . . army* Another reference to the battle of Marathon (see the Glossary, and the preceding note).

462 *Athens, remembering* Here, and again at 1352, Aeschylus seems ironically to put into a Persian mouth an allusion to the story that after the Athenian attack on Sardis (401-5, note) King Darius was so incensed that he ordered a servant to repeat three times, every time he dined: "My Lord, remember Athens!" The first extant version of the anecdote may be read in Herodotus, V.105.

508-23 *kept butting . . . immigrant* Again, as in 401-5, there is doubt as to the correct order of the lines; and here a case can also be made for the theory that one or two lines have been entirely lost. Certainty does not seem possible, but we have adopted what seems to us the likeliest order of the many possible orders that have been suggested.

516 *from a golden city*   The Greek here has the adjective *Chryseus*, which strictly should mean "belonging to the (town of) Chrysa." The only Chrysa generally known to antiquity was an insignificant town in the neighborhood of Troy (cf. *Iliad* I.37), but this seems an improbable residence for a Persian divisional general; we therefore prefer, with several commentators, to believe that Aeschylus has here simply invented an exotic-sounding Persian place-name. The glint of gold (Greek *chrysos*) in it may not be in any way accidental; J. L. comments: "This is the last reference to gold in the play. Here its light winks out."

571-3 *Gods keep . . . can't be shaken*   The city of Athens, of course, had been sacked in the campaign preceding the naval battle, and indeed was to be sacked again in the following year (see the Introduction, pp. 8–9), but it would scarcely have been in human nature for an Athenian dramatist to have labored this point before an Athenian audience. Aeschylus neatly has the Messenger avoid this admission by citing a thought which had long been current among Greek writers, in various forms: *not walls, but people, make a city*. He may have in mind the rather similar retort made by the great Athenian leader Themistokles, just before the battle, to one who taunted him with having lost his city (Herodotus, VIII.61).

579-94 *My lady . . . high jealousy*   Perhaps more clearly than any other single passage in the play, this illustrates the difference between our poet's vision of the events, and the vision of a historian. Underlying it, evidently, is the same incident that Herodotus recorded a generation or so later (VIII.75-6): Themistokles, seeing that the Greek fleet as a whole was bent on retreating from the anchorage at Salamis to cover the Peloponnese, sent a household slave of his, Sikinnos, to the Persian fleet. As instructed, Sikinnos persuaded the Persian admirals that Themistokles secretly wished them to succeed, and was therefore letting them know that the Greek fleet was panicking and preparing to sail away out of their grasp. The Persians therefore disposed their ships to block the exits from the straits during that same night. By this trickery

Themistokles made up the minds of the non-Athenian Greek admirals for them: like it or not, the fleet must stay where it was, and give battle in the straits. So he ensured not only that the battle would be joined in a place where the Persian numerical superiority would count for least, but also that Attica would not be irrevocably abandoned by the Greek forces.

By contrast, it will be seen that Aeschylus lets the responsibility for starting the battle float mysteriously in the interspace between Man and God; this is brought out with heavy emphasis both at the beginning and the end of the passage. To translate literally: at 581-83 the anonymous individual who begins it all is "a vengeance-spirit (*alastor*) or an evil *daimon* who appeared from somewhere; for a Greek man, who came from the Athenian fleet . . ." (that "for," when one reflects on it, is seen to be one of the most enigmatic occurrences of the little word in literature). Then, at the close (592-94), Xerxes "as soon as he heard, not understanding the deceit of the Greek man nor yet the jealousy of the Gods," issues the orders which will bring on the battle.

What Aeschylus has done is to suppress the Greek individuals' names and personalities (just as he does throughout this play); on the Persian side, to concentrate attention on the grandiose and tragic figure of Xerxes, ignoring the anonymous Persian officers who bear the responsibility in the version known to Herodotus; and above all, to distribute the action between God and Man at the opening, and Man and God at the close.

691-3 *We might have been tuna . . . bits of wreckage* The appalling character of this image does not seem to have been fully grasped by Aeschylus' commentators. We are made to be present at a tuna round-up of the kind still to be witnessed until recently in Southern European waters. Alan Villiers, *Give Me a Ship To Sail* (New York, 1958), pp. 59–67, gives a general account, and also an eyewitness report of a round-up off Cape Santa Maria; here are some extracts, which may throw light on the Aeschylean lines. The tuna were funneled by a great barrier of nets into a kind of corral of nets and boats, within which the tuna

swims and swims, looking for a shadowless passage. There is none. He is trapped—doomed. . . . Near-naked men . . . thrust deftly with their hooks and long gaffs among the tuna, cutting at them with swift blows, the red blood spurting thick. . . . Great shapely blue bodies are everywhere, with wild staring eyes, and the water is soon tinged and then stained red with the tuna's blood.

707-51 *You must understand . . . butchered* In the Messenger's account, the climax of the battle is this massacre of the Persian nobles trapped on the islet. Again, Herodotus' version is worth comparing. In VIII.76 he briefly mentions that the Persian commanders, on the evening before the battle, disembarked "many of the Persians" on an islet to which he gives the name Psyttaleia, in order to intercept any shipwrecked Greeks. In VIII.95 he records with almost equal brevity how in the midst of the battle the great Athenian statesman Aristeides "took along with him many of the heavy infantry who had been stationed along the shore of Salamis, being Athenians, and conveyed them to the island of Psyttaleia, and there landed them; and they slaughtered the Persians on the islet to a man." Here is the now familiar contrast between poet and historian: Herodotus gives names and particulars, but does not render the atmosphere or the pathos as Aeschylus does. And the two authors differ profoundly in the importance that they attach to this engagement: what to Herodotus is a passing incident is the ultimate disaster in Aeschylus' account. On the evidence that we have, it is probably idle to speculate on the reasons for this; just as it seems impossible now to be sure whether Psyttaleia is to be identified with the islet known as Lipsokoutali on modern maps, lying across the mouth of the strait, or that known as St. George, within the sound. A good account of the debate on these questions is given in Broadhead's Appendix VI to his edition of our play.

752-833 *Then Xerxes . . . on Persians* This account of the aftermath of the battle differs greatly from that given by Herodotus (VIII.97-120), which is summarized in the Introduction, pp. 8-9. In part, the reason may well be that neither author possessed reliable information about the details of Xerxes' calamitous retreat to Asia; the historian, indeed, actually admits that he had heard two quite different versions of its final stage, from the River Strymōn onward (VIII.118-20). It further seems very likely, however, that Aeschylus has deliberately omitted some events, and foreshortened the course of others. He has made Xerxes retreat immediately after the battle (just as does Timotheos in his lyric poem on the battle three-quarters of a century later, and no doubt for the same artistic reasons); Herodotus, however—who should have been able to find witnesses enough to this point—makes Xerxes delay for some days in Attica. While Aeschylus brings Xerxes directly home to Susa (apparently—such is our poet's lordly attitude to mere time—still wearing the clothes that he had rent at Salamis), Herodotus has him repair to Sardis and remain there for nearly a year. Aeschylus also says nothing, in this passage, of the Persian army which was left behind to winter in northern Greece (see 1306-13, with the note there). Everything, in fact, is so arranged as to heighten the impression of immediate and total humiliation both for Xerxes and for his forces. Finally, the climax to Aeschylus' version of the retreat, the freezing and melting of the River Strymōn, is not even hinted at in Herodotus, and has seemed incredible to many commentators on meteorological grounds, if on no others.

At this distance in space and time, it is hard to decide where the factual truth of Aeschylus' story of the retreat ends, and where the poet-moralist's shaping imagination begins. But we can still admire the grim, majestic poem which he has made out of it, from 780 onward. In the Greek, these lines seem to trudge and struggle almost like the battered army itself, through a malevolent landscape which rings with names rich in the association to an ancient Greek audience; for in the evocative use of place-names Aeschylus perhaps has no equal among the European poets until Milton.

780-805 *And the army . . . bank to bank* The modern reader will not be so familiar with the geographical names in this passage as the original audience was, and we therefore give some account of them here. For a production or reading aloud of the *Persians*, some might prefer a version that cuts out the names, giving instead the associations which they might be thought to have evoked for a Greek hearer; such a version, composed by J.L., is added at the end of this note.

The army more or less retraces the route that it had taken in the spring of 480: northward through the provinces of central Greece—Boiotia, Phokis, and Doris—until they hit the sea at the Mēlian Gulf (here is Thermopylae, site of the battle, and here the River Spercheios enters the sea); then into the northern section of the Greek peninsula, passing through Phthiotic Achaia (Achilles' country, this), Thessaly, and the mountainous coastal region of Magnesia. Entering half-Greek Macedonia, they cross the River Axios at the northwest corner of the Aegean Sea, and wheel eastward into eastern Macedonia and then into Thrace—a

wild, magical landscape, best known to a Greek for its association
with the legends of Dionysos and Orpheus, which Aeschylus
himself treated in his now lost cycle of Dionysiac plays. The great
river Strymōn enters the north Aegean at a point between Lake
Bolbē and Mount Pangaios (here live the Ēdonoi, a tribe once
ruled by King Lykourgos, the early persecutor and victim of Dionysos); it is at this river, as we have seen, that Aeschylus sets the
most terrible incident of the retreat. *Alternative version of 780-
805:*

And the army left
    kept dropping off,
        first on ground a short march from Athens,
some of thirst
    taunted by bright springs
        out of exhaustion's reach,
while some of us,
    empty from panting,
drove on through plundered orchards
and fields that once held bounty, and on
    along that sea-grazed coast where
the Rapid River spills earthkindly drink.
After that hardscrabble farms
and towns in the lean north took us in
    when we were starving.
There the most died.
    Thirst and hunger,
        both of them stalked us.
And slogging on
    through high white passes
    and a wilderness of trees
we came to the Worthy's ford
and a bubbling swamp choked with reeds
and the mountain called All-Earth—
    a fox-haunted place
        that tears men apart.
It was that night
        some god
blew down winter out of season and froze
the holy Harsh River bank to bank.

850 *wine poured out with honey*   The Greek has *pelanos;* see 1339, note.

868-960 In Greek theatrical terminology, this is the first *stasimon,* i.e. the first
complete choral song after the *parodos* (1-182, and note). The

song proper actually begins at 886; it is prefaced by a passage of anapestic chant, during which the Chorus may perhaps be envisaged as moving forward in a body from the skēnē to take up position for dancing in the orchestra. If we have guessed correctly at the setting of the play (cf. the Introduction, p. 19), this move will almost be the equivalent of a scene-change in the modern theater, since it will bring the Chorus close to the tomb-mound of Darius—that is, to the focal point of the ensuing action.

The song is full of the clearly articulated wailing-words in which ancient Greek is so rich, and which are almost entirely lacking in modern English. Against English "alas!" (and even this is now an archaism), the Greek of this song alone can set *popoi*, *totoi*, *pheu*, *ē-ē*, and *o-ā*, balancing each other with antiphonal effect. Direct translation of them being impossible, this version seeks to render them by repetitions of phrases and by concentration on long vowel-sounds.

868 God The Greek has "Zeus."

873 mothers This is not in the Greek text, but was conjecturally supplied by the nineteenth-century scholar W. Dindorf.

894 riverdhows rigged for the sea The Greek has "ocean-barides," baris being a rather vague term for any non-Greek, non-seagoing vessel, especially those which plied on the Nile. The phrase, therefore, is paradoxical, and probably scornful too.

902-3 Sailwings unfurled, bluedark eyes on the sea The Greek reading in the first phrase here is uncertain; following many others, we have adopted a conjecture by the eighteenth-century scholar C. G. Schütz, which literally will mean "linen-winged." The second phrase is also, in the Greek, a single, magnificent compound word, which could be interpreted either as "dark-blue-faced" or as "dark-blue-eyed." We prefer the latter, recalling the eyes commonly shown painted on ships' prows in Greek vase-paintings (and still to be seen on some southern European fishing boats), as well as Aeschylus' words in Suppliant Maidens 716, where an Egyptian warship has a "prow scanning with its eyes the course ahead."

922 Salamis Here the Greek has "the Kychreian shore." Kychreus was an ancient hero-king of Salamis, of whose legend not much is now known.

According to a relatively late source, Pausanias (*Description of Greece*, I.36.1), he manifested himself during the battle of Salamis, in the guise of a snake; it is not impossible that this story was already current in Aeschylus' time, and that this phrase is therefore a muted allusion to it.

961-1001 By the received terminology (cf. 183-867, note), this is the second episode of the play, although in fact the action develops without a real break from 961 to 1397. Throughout, the center of attention is the tomb-mound of Darius. The Queen's change of dress and equippage (see our stage-direction before 961, which is based on the Queen's own words at 975-76) similarly emphasizes the somber and unearthly atmosphere into which the play now enters.

This is, of course, not the only occasion in Greek tragedy on which offerings and invocations are made at a tomb; compare, in particular, Aeschylus' *Libation-Bearers* 1-509 (and, for such practices in actual Greek life from the earliest times until today, Margaret Alexiou's *The Ritual Lament in Greek Tradition*, Cambridge, 1974). What makes our scene unique among the extant instances is that here, finally, the dead man actually rises up out of his grave, to the consternation of the mourners. This need by no means have been a foregone conclusion—in the *Libation-Bearers* the pleas to the dead man to return are scarcely less passionate than they are here, and yet Agamemnon does not manifest himself visibly—and the first audience of this play may well have been as shocked by the ghost's eventual appearance as are the Chorus on the dancing-floor.

995-1089 The second *stasimon*: after a few introductory lines of anapestic chanting (995-1013), the Chorus break into full song and dance. It is likely that this ghost-raising ode was accompanied by unusually violent movement; compare our tentative stage-direction at 1053, and our note at 1094-95.

1004 *Soul-Guide* Hermes (one of whose many aspects is that of *Psychopompos*, Escort of Souls) is named in the Greek.

1037 *tomb* Here and at 1057 the word used for this in the Greek is *ochthos*, literally "tomb-mound."

1039, 1042 *Hand of Death* In both places the Greek text has *Aidoneus*, an old poetic name for the god Hades.

1054 *Shah* Here Aeschylus uses a rare and strange word, *Balēn;* the ancient Greek writers themselves, while agreeing that it meant "King," were uncertain about its origin, but the balance of the evidence seems to favor the theory that it belongs to an Oriental language. On some views, it is to be connected with *Baal* and *Beelzebub.* This stanza is, indeed, heavily Oriental; Darius' clothing also, as specified in the ensuing lines, is the characteristic clothing of a King of Kings.

1082-83 *now mourn . . . exciting old?* The Greek words here are hopelessly corrupt; we can offer no more than a guess at the original meaning.

1089 *ships . . . ghostships* Greek has a negativing prefix a-, roughly equivalent to English un-. Aeschylus here writes *naes* "ships," and follows it with a unique adjective, apparently invented for the occasion, *a-naes.* On this fearful note he ends his ode.

1090-1397 The third episode (cf. 183-867, note).

1094-95 *The earth . . . scratched open* All the Greek manuscripts give a text which will translate, word for word: "moans, has been struck, and is being scratched the earth." Students of Aeschylus have long debated whether this text can be correct, what is the subject of the first two verbs (all seem to agree that the subject of the third one is "the earth"), and what is the meaning of the statement as a whole. Without claiming certainty, we believe that the best solution is to take "the earth" as the subject of all three verbs—the flow of the line in Greek seems very much in favor of this—and to take those verbs in their literal senses. We assume that they describe the activities of the Chorus during, and perhaps just after, the preceding ode (cf. our stage-direction before 1054). For the ghastly detail of the scratching at the earth, one might possibly compare the Roman poet Horace's parody of a ghost-raising ritual (*Satires* I.8.26-27), where the necromancers "score the earth with their nails"; although there the object seems to be to open up a pit for blood-offerings.

1171-94 *How? Thunderbolts . . . There is no doubt* The dead Darius is by now so far detached from life on earth, and so near divinity, that he knows nothing of the recent actions of Xerxes and of the Persian forces. Only after Atossa has informed him of the expedition and

its defeat at Salamis is he able to connect the news with his supernatural knowledge of the doom stored up in Heaven (1195-1203,
1312-16): the folly of taming the Hellespont and crossing the
water to invade Greece, whenever it takes place, must entail a
Salamis and, beyond that, a Plataia.

Aeschylus is not the only great poet who has attributed this
selective vision to the dead. As the great Dutch commentator,
Groeneboom, notes on this scene, the inhabitants of the Inferno
are somewhat similarly described: we can dimly see events that
are to come on earth, says the shade of Farinata degli Uberti, "but
when they are near, or are, our intelligence is vain" (compare the
whole passage, Inf.X.94-108).

1188 *even the old ones* So says the Greek text; it is almost certainly corrupt—
would aged Bactrians have been drafted into the expedition?—
but no convincing emendation has been put forward.

1256 *the greatest* We translate literally here; but the reader should bear in mind
that in the Greek poets, conscious as they were of the law of
hybris and *ātē*, "greatness" in human beings and their works is
usually a sinister attribute.

1265-94 *The Mede . . . devastation* To emphasize by contrast the folly of Xerxes
and the heights from which the Persian realm has so suddenly
fallen, Aeschylus puts into the ghost's mouth a review of the line
of earlier kings. There are some doubts in this passage about the
readings, the order of the lines, and the identification of one or
two of the monarchs. These doubts—most of which are not finally
resolvable on present evidence, and none of which affect the general effect of the speech—are well discussed by Broadhead in his
commentary, especially in his Supplementary Note on pp. 278-79.
Here we need only remark that, following most editors, we have
omitted a line which occurs in the manuscripts after 1281, "and
sixth was Maraphis, seventh Artaphrenes," since 1. no such Persian kings are mentioned in any other source and, perhaps more
decisively, 2. it seems next to impossible to squeeze two monarchs
in between the assassination of Mardos and the accession of
Darius. The line may be a fragment of an ancient comment,
mutilated and mistakenly worked into the poetic text.

The names mentioned in the speech are explained in the
Glossary.

1306-11 *But you must . . . from Europe?* The important fact that a Persian army had remained in Greece after Xerxes' flight was omitted from the Messenger's narrative, no doubt on account of dramatic considerations (cf. 752-833, note). Only here does the ghost— relying, as he says in the following lines, on the information provided by the divine oracles—reveal it to the Chorus.

1330-31 *shrines . . . the undying Dead* The Greek has "shrines of the *daimones*"; the translator has accepted the theory favored by some commentators that this is Aeschylus' way of saying "tombs," since in a few specialized contexts the dead may be called *daimones*.

1336-37 *wellspring . . . unchecked* The reading of the Greek here is evidently corrupt. We have tentatively accepted the emendation made by the scholar-poet A. E. Housman. Its merits are that it introduces not merely an image that is fine in itself, but an image that seems to have been near the surface of Aeschylus' consciousness anyway, during the composition of this play; compare the "fountain of silver" at 405, and the "fountain of defeats" at 1207.

1339 *sacrifices of clotting blood* The Greek has "bloodslaughtered *pelanos*," which may provide yet another instance of Aeschylus' manipulation of words and their meanings through the course of a play. *Pelanos* is used in Greek to refer to certain substances that are viscous, on the borderline between liquid and solid. Most often it is found in ritual and sacrificial contexts, to mean offerings of meal and honey, or of blended liquids. At 324, and again at 850, Atossa has spoken of offering a *pelanos*, in this ritual sense, to the supernatural powers, to avert disaster. Here the word occurs for the last time in the play, but in another well-established sense: of a sticky clot of blood.

1341 *Dorian spears* Although the Athenians were present in force at the battle of Plataia, it was the Dorian Greeks of the Peloponnese, and above all the Spartans, who played the greatest part in the victory. This line seems to pay tribute to that fact.

1359-60 *Because . . . himself* The reading is uncertain. We have doubtfully followed Broadhead's text (which adopts a reading found in a minority of the manuscript witnesses) and interpretation.

1379-83 *give joy to your souls . . . the dead* Darius' parting words have worried many readers and commentators: why this apparently hedonistic advice to his old counsellors, to conclude a series of speeches so dignified, so rich in insight into the ways of the universe? In seeking to interpret them, one should probably begin from the fact that *Darius here speaks in the authentic language of the dead*—that is, of the pagan dead. He expresses an understanding of death and life—the finality of the one, the limitations imposed on the other—which not only permeates Greek poetry from Homer onward, but is also formulated with an especial poignancy in many a pagan epitaph, both Greek and Roman. Broadhead's commentary cites a number of examples. One could add more, like this (from a Roman tombstone): "See, I lie in my tomb and I have no feeling; I warn you, enjoy, while life is given you!" Or this (from a Greek tombstone of Roman imperial date): "I, Euodos, give this advice to all mortals: let your soul have a share of pleasure [cf. 1379 here], knowing that if once you go down to the stream of Lethe you will never see, there below, anything of what is above." Darius, like the plebeian dead who speak to the passers-by in such epitaphs, has a double message; of which the one component, the advice to enjoy what life we have, seems but a foil to the other, which is the utter hopelessness and finality of death. It is that cloud, we are reminded as the royal ghost sinks back into the tomb, that hangs over all human endeavor: over the Persian expedition, and over the Persian accumulation of wealth, *ploutos*, which word occurs here for the last time in the play.

1398-1469 The third *stasimon*; in the Greek, this song stands out among all the other songs in the *Persians* because it is composed almost entirely in the magnificent dactylic rhythm, which may have had heroic connotations for a Greek hearer (the dactylic hexameter is, of course, the metre of the Homeric epics). Certainly the content is heroic, or heroizing. It is an evocation of the effortless power of the dead Darius, bitterly contrasted in the final lines (1463-69) with the calamity that Xerxes' efforts have brought upon the Persian empire. The core of the ode is the great roll-call of cities and islands (1418-62) which, say the Chorus, Darius caused to be conquered without ever stirring from his own fireside, and without ever a reverse to the Persian army. (All these places, as a matter of history, were lost to the empire after the failure of the expedition, and in the very period of this play the Athenians were recruiting them into a naval league which in time was to become an empire itself.)

Comparison with the historical evidence about Darius' reign suggests that Aeschylus has either knowingly suppressed certain particulars of it, or (as is quite possible in some cases, given the date and place at which he composed) knew little or nothing about them. For instance, one of the most extensive episodes in Herodotus' account of the reign is the Scythian Expedition (IV. 1-144), in which, so far from sitting on the far side of the Halys River, Darius marched from Susa to the Thracian Bosporos, *threw a bridge across it*, threw a second bridge across the Danube, and penetrated far into southern Russia, from which he was obliged to retreat with considerable danger and humiliation. As so often in the study of this play, we have to remind ourselves that Aeschylus does not set out to compose history, but poetry. As so often also, we may find in the last analysis that his poetic intuition, his sense of the underlying realities, is not so wide of the historical truth after all. The *general* contrast drawn in this ode between the reigns and personalities of Darius and Xerxes is in accord with the general tenor of Herodotus' accounts of them, and of the other evidence.

1398 *GOD, PITY US* The Greek has an exclamation of anguish, not directly translatable.

1412 *The laws . . . on towers* The correct reading and interpretation of this line are hotly, and quite inconclusively, debated. Our translation renders the apparent meaning of the Greek words offered in nearly all the manuscripts, but we are not confident they are anything like the words which Aeschylus originally wrote here.

1419 *the Halys river* The Halys runs into the Black Sea midway along the northern coast of Asia Minor, and was the ancient boundary between western Asia Minor and the kingdoms further east (Herodotus, I.6 and 72; compare also the story of the sixth-century Lydian king Croesus' fatal crossing of it from west to east, *ibid.* 75-91).

1422-31 *the Rivergod's cities . . . Black Sea's mouth* This first section of the survey of Darius' conquests in the Aegean area covers the coastal region of the province called Thrace in ancient times. It begins from the neighborhood of the River Strymōn at Thrace's western border, and then ranges eastward to the Hellespont, the Propontis (Sea of Marmara) and the Thracian Bosporos (the strait between the Propontis and the Black Sea). So much is clear, but there are the gravest doubts about the details of all but the last three lines. The text offered by most of the manuscripts in 1422-27, literally translated, runs approximately: "(cities) such as those of Acheloos [a river-god] belonging to the Strymōnian water-expanse, neighboring the Thracian settlements; and those outside the lake, along the dry land, with fortifications running around them; these listened to him as lord." Some think that the "cities of Acheloos" can be identified with the lake-dweller settlements on the lower Strymōn, described by Herodotus (V.16).

It will be noted that the Chorus' survey begins from the very region at which the Messenger's detailed narrative broke off (820). This is surely deliberate: by the play's end the hearer will have traversed a poetic map of the entire theater of the Greco-Persian wars.

1432-55 *And wave-caressed . . . our groans* Now comes a long list of islands—their names, perhaps, being more evocative to Aeschylus' first audience than to a modern reader, for during the years since Xerxes' defeat Athenian squadrons had been constantly cruising these very waters. The exposition is not so orderly as in the previous section of the survey, as a glance at a map of the Aegean will show, but there are fewer obscurities in detail. First come three important islands close to the Asian mainland, Lesbos, Chios, and Samos; then the isles of the Cyclades, Paros . . . Andros; then an oddly assorted group, Lemnos sitting solitary in the middle of the North Aegean, Icaria (presumably meant by "Ikaros' settling place," 1448) well to the south, Rhodes off southwest Asia Minor, and Knidos (an interesting error, for Knidos is no island, but sits on the end of a slender tongue of land projecting from the continent; had Aeschylus only seen it from the sea?). Then comes Cyprus, with three of its major cities mentioned by name; appropriately, the last is Cyprian Salamis, which legend held to be a daughter-city of Athenian Salamis (see the Glossary, under AJAX).

1456-62 *And more . . . a thousand tribes* The survey ends with the mainland province of Ionia, stretching along the central portion of the western coast of Asia Minor, and perhaps the bitterest loss of all for the Persians to bear. Since Cyrus' time, with a brief interlude of revolt in the opening years of the fifth century, this land, with its many rich and populous Greek cities, had been a Persian fief. In Xerxes' expedition many Ionian Greeks, whether they liked it or not, had served on the Persian side; now they too, like the Greeks of the islands, were free.

1470-1714 The concluding section of the tragedy, following the last complete *stasimon:* the *exodos,* in the terminology which we have received from Aristotle. In the *Persians* the *exodos* contains not a single line in unaccompanied speech. The opening passage, at Xerxes' entry (1470-89), is in chanted anapests. At 1490 the character both of the metre and of the dialect used in the Greek suggest that the style of delivery changes, almost certainly to the level of full song. From 1506 until the end of the play there is no question that everyone is singing, and presumably dancing as well. The reader of the play in English will be able to observe for himself how the tempo quickens: at first Xerxes and the Chorus exchange fairly lengthy passages, but they end by exchanging single lines (and indeed, in two passages, probably half-lines only). In all Greek tragedy there is only one other such totally operatic, antiphonal *exodos,* and that is in Aeschylus' next surviving dated play, the *Seven Against Thebes* of 467 B.C. (if we assume, as many students do, that the passage 1005 ff. there is probably by a later hand).

For the translator, the problem becomes similar to that already presented by the choral ode 868-960 (compare the end of the note on that passage). As J. L. writes: in the Greek

verbally meaningful lines yield to lines in which rhythm and sheer sound carry the messages. There is a heavy emphasis in the translation on these sounds: long o, long a, oo, ow, and long e. Certain words, such as sorrow and gone, are repeated often in an attempt to capture the repeated howls and cries in the text.

But even when the translator's task has been carried out as sensitively as it has been here, the reader who would do proper honor to the poet's conception must also labor for his part to hear and see this climax to the play, where all the performing arts finally merged: verbal, musical, choreographic, and scenic.

1470 The stage-direction before this line is based on what seems to us the most probable interpretation of lines 1620-25, which read literally: "I marvel, I marvel at them [the lost Persian soldiers] not following behind you, around the tent drawn on wheels." There is little doubt that this passage describes the vehicle called the *harmamaxa*, a kind of caravan *de luxe*, in which Xerxes did in fact occasionally ride during his expedition (Herodotus, VII.41). Commentators debate whether the vehicle would actually have appeared on the scene at this point. In concluding that it did, we have borne in mind the Queen's original entry in a chariot (194, note); the contrast and parallel to it which would be produced by the appearance of Xerxes in a *harmamaxa* here; the importance of the yoke-image in this play; and Aeschylus' standing tendency to create symbolic visual effects. The other points in the stage-direction, however, should be taken as guesses only. Another guess relates to the exact point at which Xerxes will descend from the vehicle (see the stage-direction before 1506). That, whenever he first comes into the audience's view, he will be pitifully dressed in torn clothes, is made certain by 1370-71, 1391-92, 1646, 1660.

1474-75 *some undying Lust . . . Persia's clans* The Greek reads, literally: "how rawheartedly a *daimon* stamped on the race of the Persians!"

1481 *Dear God* The Greek has "Zeus!".

1489 *deathless Power* The Greek has, again, *daimon*.

1493 *maw of Death* The Greek has Hades, the God.

1513-18 *bleak howls . . . promise you* The Greek has, literally: ". . . I will send, I will send you the cry ominously uttered, the howl well versed in evil, of a Mariandynan keener." The Mariandynoi, a tribe of Asia Minor, were known for the passionate and unrestrained kind of mourning which they practiced in their tribal cult. Aeschylus' allusion to them may well be taken as a hint to future directors about the style of song and dance that he intended for this last section of the play. A similar hint may be incorporated at 1688 (see the note there).

1524 *Heaven* The Greek has *daimon*.

1540 *black as night plain* This seems to be a riddle, very much in Aeschylus' manner, for the expanse of sea off Salamis.

1542-1625 *Thousands . . . carriage wheels* This passage is the third and last of the three long roll-calls of Persian commanders that span our play. In the first (28-68) we hear of them in all their pride and pomp, marching against Greece; in the second (494-540) their varied deaths are narrated by the Messenger; in the third the names are heard through a storm of wailing. In translating the long stanzas of the Greek (each stanza divided between Xerxes and the Chorus, the Chorus taking the larger share), the translator has rendered the Greek fairly freely, for here above all it is a matter of responding *sounds*. Thus the long drawn out "Thousands the thousands!", and the refrain "WHERE ARE THEY NOW?", for instance, are her additions—but additions made for rhythmic ends not unlike those at which Aeschylus seems to have aimed. As a model, she has had in mind the *ubi sunt*, an ancient device used in the lamentations of many times and countries; for example, in the Anglo-Saxon *Erdstoppa* (Where is the horse? Where is the man? Where is the giver of treasure?); or in the twelfth-century passion play, the *Planctus Mariae* (*Ubi sunt discipuli? Ubi sunt apostoli?*).

1587-88 *Your most faithful . . . Eye* This is very probably a reference to an official Persian title, "Eye of the King," of which we know otherwise from a hilarious episode in Aristophanes' comedy, the *Acharnians* (91-125), and from a sober mention in Xenophon's *Cyropaedia* (VIII.2.10). Holders of the office were apparently confidential agents who reported directly to the King.

1592 *you left HIM there* This line is conjectural; the Greek metres show that a line has been lost from the text here.

1614 *nomads* The Greek has *Mardoi*; Herodotus mentions them (I.125) as being a nomadic clan of the Persians.

1622-25 *They'll not . . . carriage wheels* See 1470, note, for a discussion of this passage.

1626 *Gone, the leaders* At this point there is a sudden change in the character of the singing. From now until the end of the play Xerxes and the Chorus for the most part exchange line for line, instead of part-stanza for part-stanza; the metre becomes overwhelmingly iambo-trochaic (this is that same lament-rhythm which was heard in the final section of the parodos, 149-82); and, perhaps most interestingly, Xerxes gradually assumes more and more initiative in the singing. Instead of being the mere target for near-insults and pointed questions directed at him by the Chorus, he becomes first a partner in the lament and then, from 1668 onward, its conductor, issuing instructions which the Chorus dutifully obey. There does not seem to be enough evidence to allow one to do more than speculate on Aeschylus' dramatic motive in causing this near-reversal of roles. Possibly the intention might be to remind us that under the Persian system, as Atossa remarked long ago, *Xerxes still reigns*, however much he has abused his charge; in the last resort he is not accountable to any earthly auditor (343, note). And indeed, it is almost never without a shock that one recalls, on emerging from the dramatic illusion created in the *Persians*, that when it was first performed Xerxes was still alive and holding court in one of his great throne-halls, whether in Susa or in that whose ruins still survive at Persepolis.

With the change in the singing comes increased stage-business, culminating in the wild breast-beating, hair-tearing, and robe-rending of 1678-97.

1630 *Undying Powers*   The Greek is *daimones*.

1632 *Blind Folly*   The Greek is *ātē*. We are reminded here, and again at 1643 (where "Great Fool" represents a word meaning approximately "greatly beset by *ātē*), of the interlude in the *parodos*, 137-48.

1688 *crooning wails*   The Greek has, literally, "and cry in accompaniment, in the Mysian style." The Mysians, a people of Asia Minor, were known, like the Mariandynoi (1513-19, note), for their passionate manner of mourning. Again, this may be an indication of the way in which the poet wished this last scene to be delivered and acted.

GLOSSARY

Note: Two groups of names have been omitted from this glossary. First are the very numerous geographical names which occur—most of them on one occasion only—in the Messenger's narrative of the Persian retreat (780-805), and in the choral ode on the conquests of Darius (1398-1469); they are explained in the Notes on those passages. Second is the even more numerous group of names of Persian warriors in the three "roll-calls" (see the note on 1542-1625). Relatively few of these names occur more than once in the play; some of them are thought actually to have been invented by Aeschylus; and even where a name can be shown to be genuinely Persian, and to occur in Herodotus' lists of the Persians involved in the expedition, identifications are not often certain. In short, it seems likely that even Aeschylus and his audience would in most cases have known little more about them than we do. There thus seemed to be no point in loading the Notes or Glossary with repeated entries of the type: "*Egdadatas:* name of a Persian known only from *Persians* 1618." What little definite information is known about the Persian names—and it is information of more importance to Indo-European philologists and professional historians than to the reader who is interested in Aeschylean poetic drama—is conveniently assembled in Appendix V to Broadhead's edition of our play.

AJAX, the hero made famous in Homer's epics and in Sophocles' great play, appears in the *Persians* only in his capacity of patron saint, as it were, of the island of Salamis. According to Greek legend, both he and his father Telamon resided there; and it was his younger brother, Teucer, who after the Trojan War colonized the other Salamis, in Cyprus.

ARTAPHRENES, a Persian noble, described in 1279 as having been a leader in the conspiracy to assassinate the usurper Mardos in 521 B.C. He is probably identical with the individual whom Herodotus names Intaphrenes in his story of that conspiracy (III.70, 78). See also under MARDOS. (A different Artaphrenes is named among the Persian warriors at line 29.)

ATOSSA, Queen Mother of the Persian realm. She was a daughter of Cyrus the Great, and was married three times: first to her brother Cambyses, then to the usurper Mardos, and finally to Darius (Herodotus, III.88). She was evidently a powerful character: Herodotus (III.134 and VII.3) emphasizes her influence over Darius, especially in persuading him to designate their son Xerxes as his successor to the empire. By the time of the great expedition of 480 she must have been well on in years, since her first husband had died as long ago as 522 B.C.

Such is the biography of Atossa that can be gathered from Herodotus' history. How much of it was known to Aeschylus or his audience, and indeed whether they were even familiar with her name, is uncertain; for this question, see 194, note.

BACTRIA, one of the furthest eastern provinces of the Persian empire, in the region between the River Oxus and the range of the Hindu Kush. Bactrian infantry and cavalry contingents served in Xerxes' expedition (Herodotus VII. 64, 86).

BOSPOROS, as used in this play (1179, 1215), this name refers to the Hellespont (Dardanelles). In most other Greek writers it means the "Thracian Bosporos," the strait which joins the Sea of Marmara to the Black Sea; but there are a few exceptions, similar to this.

CILICIANS (538), inhabitants of the region that lies along the southern coast of Asia Minor.

CYRUS, called The Great, is referred to in lines 1268-74. In effect the founder of the Persian empire (cf. the Introduction,

pp. 5–6), he ruled from 559 to 529 B.C., and was succeeded by his son Cambyses. The latter—perhaps because his character and reputation were so disastrous, at
least as the Greeks perceived them—is not expressly named
in Darius' account of the Persian Kings, but is alluded to
merely as "Cyrus' son" in line 1275. Cambyses' reign (described in Herodotus, III.1-65) lasted from 529 to 522 B.C.

DARIUS ascended the Persian throne in 521 B.C., after the assassination of the usurper Mardos (q.v.), and ruled until he died
in 486 B.C. He belonged to a collateral branch of the same
royal house, the Achaemenids, as did Cyrus. Taking
Atossa as his chief wife, he was by her the father of Xerxes.
His reign marks the climax of the Persian empire; he or-
ganized the administration of the territories won under
Cyrus and Cambyses, and added greatly to them. All the
historical sources indicate that he was a wise and, on the
whole, magnanimous ruler, although his reign was less
serene, and less unbrokenly successful in war, than the
Persians would have us believe (cf. 1398-1469, note).

EKBATANA (the most familiar spelling of the name, which we have
adopted; the manuscript evidence indicates that Aeschylus
actually spelled it Agbatana), modern Hamadan, was the
capital city of the Medes (q.v.). Built with great splendor
by the Median king Deiokes (according to Herodotus,
I.98), it continued to be an important center, and one of
the royal residences, under the Persian empire.

HELLĒ, according to ancient legend, Hellē and her brother Phrixos
were the children of a king of Boiotia, Athamas, and of
his first wife Nephelē. When Athamas remarried, Nephelē
tried to save the children from the plots of their wicked
stepmother by mounting them on a ram with a golden
fleece, which bore them away from Greece through the
sky. Hellē fell from the ram into the straits now called the
Dardanelles, which thence obtained the name "Sea of
Hellē," Hellespontos.

KISSA, a "Kissian land" is known to Herodotus (III.91, etc.) as a
district in the neighborhood of the Persian capital, Susa;

123

contingents of its inhabitants, Kissians, marched in Xerxes' army (VII.62, 86). It may be yet another instance of the deficiencies in the information available to Aeschylus about Persia, that he evidently believes in the existence of a walled city, Kissa, comparable with Ekbatana and Susa in importance.

LYDIANS, Lydia was the territory inland of the Ionian Greek colonies which occupied the central shoreline of western Asia Minor. A rich and powerful kingdom in the seventh and early sixth centuries B.C., it had been conquered by Cyrus (line 1271); thereafter, according to Herodotus (I.155-6), the Lydians had succumbed to the delights of the easy life, a belief alluded to in lines 54-55 of the Persians. Its capital was Sardis (q.v.).

MARATHON, on the northeast coast of Attica, was the scene of the defeat of a seaborne expedition dispatched by Darius against the Athenians in 490 B.C. (Herodotus, VI.94-120). This great Athenian triumph is mentioned in Persians 769, and alluded to in 401, 409.

MARDOS, the name given in line 1276 to the usurper of the Persian throng whose rule intervened between those of Cambyses and Darius (q.v.) in 522-21 B.C. "Mardos" is evidently Aeschylus' spelling of the name which appears as "Smerdis" in Herodotus. In one of the most dramatic passages of his entire Histories (III.61-79), Herodotus tells how this Smerdis, one of the priestly caste called the Magi, impersonated Cambyses' dead brother (who happened to bear the same name), and ruled until he was assassinated by a group of seven Persian grandees, including Darius and Intaphrenes (? = Aeschylus' Artaphrenes, q.v.). By an extraordinary maneuver (III.84-87), Darius then secured the kingdom for himself.

MEDE, (1.) Media, an ancient kingdom to the northwest of Persia, was always joined in a close political association with it; thus, after the foundation of the empire, the names "Medes" and "Persians" come to be bracketed together in the inscriptions of the Persian kings and in Greek and Hebrew writers. "Mede" may be used to refer to either nation or both, as for instance in Persians 1300 and the

Book of Daniel, V.38 ("and Darius the Median took the kingdom").

(2.) In Darius' list of earlier kings, the first is simply described as *Mēdos*, "Mede" (1265). It is not clear whether Aeschylus meant this as an adjective or as a proper name, but in any case the king concerned is generally thought to be the man known to Herodotus as Kyaxares, who ruled Media in the years around 600 B.C. His son (mentioned, but not named, in lines 1266-67) will then be Astyages, whom the Persian Cyrus defeated, thus bringing the two kingdoms together under Persian sovereignty. The story of these kings and events may be read in Herodotus, I.95-130.

MYSIA is a territory in Asia Minor immediately north of Lydia (q.v.): Persians 69, 531, and 1688, note.

PHOENICIANS (672), these dwellers on the shoreline of central Palestine, with their age-old maritime expertise, naturally provided Xerxes with his largest naval contingent (Herodotus, VII.89, etc.). From one of their famous seaports, Tyre, they might also be referred to as "Tyrians" (1558).

PHRYGIA, a large territory in Asia Minor, the boundaries of which fluctuated considerably in ancient times; in the period of our play most of it lay in central Asia Minor, east of Mysia and Lydia.

PLATAIA (1341), a small Greek city-state just beyond the northwest border of Attica. Near it was fought the great land battle of 479 B.C.

SALAMIS, (1.) The famous island off the west coast of Attica. Aeschylus in this play also refers to it as the "isle of Ajax" (see AJAX), and as "Kychreian" (922, note). (2.) A city in Cyprus (see AJAX).

SARDIS, the ancient capital of Lydia (q.v.). Renowned for its wealth and power under the native Lydian kings, it continued to be an important city after Cyrus' conquest, when it became the seat of the Persian satraps (governors) of the region.

SILENIAI (496), the name of that stretch of the coast of Salamis Island which looked toward the location of the naval battle.

SUSA (we adopt the most familiar spelling; in Greek it is Sousa), the city in which the action of our play is set. It was the greatest of the royal cities, lying in the northwestern part of ancient Persia. Cyrus made it the administrative capital of the empire, but Darius seems to have been the first to build there on a large scale; his palace at Susa is said to have excelled even that at Persepolis (Strabo, *Geography*, XV.729).

TYRIAN, see PHOENICIANS.

XERXES, son of Darius and Atossa; he inherited the Persian throne from his father in 486 B.C. As Aeschylus was aware (cf. 1626, note), the disastrous outcome of his expedition to Greece in 480-79 B.C. in no way meant the end of his reign: he continued in office until 465 B.C., when he was assassinated by the captain of his bodyguard, and was succeeded by his son Artaxerxes.

CPSIA information can be obtained at www.ICGtesting.com
Printed in the USA
BVOW08s0921110715

408118BV00001B/3/P